CHANGING TIMES

The Writers' Circle of St. Croix

Anthology Three

Here's to inner beauty
everyone can see.

Maud

ISBN-13: 978-1480002494
ISBN-10: 1480002496

Foreword

What a treat from this lively band of wordsmiths and storytellers! This volume, *Changing Times* is the third in a series, following *Other Times, Other Cultures* in 2006 and *Limin' Times* in 2009. It is a treasure of styles and voices, of travel in place and time, of celebrations of St. Croix and of life and beauty.

Brace yourself, however. These Writers know no bounds. They will tear at your heart: in the Maroons, in long lost love, with the secret tragedy of a family's immigration, in coping with the slow death of a loved one, in facing the fading of abilities in old age, and through earthquake and the aftermath of a massacre. Yet be not afraid, these are done with grace and love, and lead us not into depression. Well, I admit that Roz's story *Invisible Friend* is downright spooky.

There are travel stories that will tickle your fancy and funny bone: Marcia on a Moroccan road trip from hell, Preston on a crazy business adventure in Trinidad, and a Nova Scotian red squirrel's religious interpretation as I trucked him across the breadth of Canada and down the west coast of the US to his "heaven" in California.

Patricia gives us three fine examples of medieval poetry forms applied to Crucian subjects, Al contributes another of his clever Sherlock Holmes tales, this one solving a murder in Danish St. Croix in the early 1900s, and Maud confesses the intimacies of an unusual love affair.

Enjoy!   *-- Don Cox*

CONTENTS

Acknowledgments

The members of the Writers' Circle of Saint Croix in the Virgin Islands would like to thank Maud Pierre Charles for her cover art work, Rosamond Hughes for editorial work, Alvin Rymsha and Don Cox for their technological help, and all our members who contributed and helped bring this book to print.

POETRY

The Writers' Circle of St. Croix

Trees of Saint Croix
A Triolet

The hills of Saint Croix are bordered by trees,
Its shorelines shaped by pendulous palms.
The flamboyant's fires are fed by the breeze.
The hills of Saint Croix are bordered by trees,

Tibbett and tamarind augment the frieze.
Manchineels maimed in storms recover in calms.
The hills of Saint Croix are bordered by trees,
Its shorelines shaped by pendulous palms.

-- Patricia Gill

The Island Deer
A Rondeau

The Island deer that grace the hill
An ancient prophecy fulfill
When knights of old in ages past
Found here their paradise at last
A peace that faiths instill.

Leaving behind the hates that kill.
They brought the deer. With us still,
--despite the flags that changed so fast-
The island deer.

As if four centuries stood still
They survived the sugar and the mill.
Outlasted time, that iconoclast
Of dreams of an Eden unsurpassed.
Let them wander as they will.
The island deer.

-- Patricia Gill

Requiem
Rondeau redoublé

Time's passed since we lived by the sea.
We danced till stars faded away.
Our laughter meant that we were free,
Unafraid we met each new day.

I remember, what more to say?
Remember how things used to be,
Hear the beat of drums as they play.
Time's passed since we lived by the sea.

Carefree friends have now ceased to be.
Joy abandoned. Try as I may
For more, there's just one memory.
We danced till stars faded away.

Hard to believe we were so gay,
That ardor became cold debris.
For when the world still went our way,
Our laughter meant that we were free.

I mourn what was not meant to be
Oft pretend that fate went astray.
Yet the sun still brightens the sea.
Unafraid we met each new day.

Something may linger, some thought stay,
Some short phrase remind you of me.
If I find words perhaps you may
Remember how things used to be.
Time's passed.

-- Patricia Gill

Dandelion

What is it in the human soul that wishes for some other?
Another path, another goal, another face, another...
Surrounded in a verdant land with flowers so exotic
How can the quest for simpler bliss be more than quixotic?

If dandelions were few to find in their symmetric splendor
If such perfected petaled disc were found in another flower
If simple taste was sought by all with equalized endeavor
Then all would claim perfection's proof without attempting
further.

If easier paths were not suspect for tempting easier decisions,
If facile truths could stand the test of deeper contemplations
Then what could flowers teach the mind about such simple
pleasures?
Then why should life persist in seeking increased and
complex treasures?

Yet dandelions have a second act, so strange in
contemplation
To sprout a throng of gossamer shrouds, its way of
transformation
Each carrying a seed below, suspended in search of finding
Some favored spot, by choice of wind, so kindly to its kind.

Then we as witnesses might conclude a similar demand
To reach, to grow, to soar beyond a prospect preordained
To find ourselves beyond belief with simpler understanding
Of what achieved, of what perceived, of what and where our
ending.

-- Richard Arnon Mathews

Maroon Race:
For Grandma Grace

Your picture
broke my
heart when
I saw it yesterday,

you were bent
over cane, your
shirt cut by a knife
straight down
to your waist

My heart broke,
Grandma Grace,
for you that day.
You told me how
he ripped your heart
raped your soul

Not the first
time he
brought you upstairs.

How you left
- did he love? –
we still
learning more…

Child growing
inside, to
be born
on the Annaly shore.

-- Priscilla Schneider

Grandma Grace

I look in your eyes,
see my past,
my dark ancestors,
- yours, too –

I see you remembering
the dream, the free flight,
to caves
and waterfalls

Dear heart-mama,
you ask me how I know
my past when I was
yet unborn,

How I know
these hills – landmarks –
our shared past,
our lives so torn

'I only see from
an inside place',
that's what I tell
my Grandma Grace.

-- Priscilla Schneider

Grace, Maroon

Her knowing eyes of amber,
her cheekbones dark and smooth
with limbs of strength
and courage, Grace
runs toward the truth

Grace – victim of
the master – lover of his son –
escaping through the kasha,
and, silently
she runs

She joins the Maroons waiting
just talks
when wind is right
no drum or babies crying
can echo in the night

The quiet cliffs of Annaly
holds essence of our kin
more precious than king sugar
and honed from
strength within

They say this island kingdom
has memories in the earth
mirages
hot and pulsing,
with spirits and rebirth

The stones we find
are markers
- to the history of our land –
Crucian mysteries, revelations
prisms ground into the sand
                    -- Priscilla Schneider

Grace: Song for My Son

A part of
my heart
beats within you;

it culled the
best, your
very essence…

from me –
and him…
but you:
more part
of me

we have
vanished from
his sight
I was carrying you
in my belly that night

He will never
find us here
by the north shore's
cliffs, steep and sheer.

And you and
I will
always
be free

on this island's
shore, by
the cliffs
and the sea.

-- Priscilla Schneider

Maroon Silence

We long for
the wind,
breeze full and steady,
coming east to west
blanketing our
sounds of life
in silence here,
at Annaly Bay

We pray
no person
hears our days
our quiet work,
with tasks unending
alive, yet with
- fear –
and beauty.

We are attuned
to all sounds:
tibbet pods' clatter
hawks' whistle,
waves' crashing power,
all season 'round
nurtured always
by our sacred ground.

-- Priscilla Schneider

Chador, Chador

In mind's eye
come images
from an
arid terrain

sand and
black veils,
women tempered
by pain

I knew
this once
years ago –
far away:

When women
are covered,
their souls
disobey.

They center
my thought,
clear my heart
for the Source.

Then, words
come unbidden
as Mind
takes its course.

-- Priscilla Schneider

Christmas Wind

The wind is
back, moaning, curling
around deck, door
and window

warm and random
unceasing motion
root-bound trees bowing
against unseen force.

Confused limbs
reach
in chaos,
- waving –

tangled
and wild,
like an
indiscriminate lover.

Undersides
of leaves
beckon forth
the rain

surcease for
a steamy island
- submitting –
cooling off again.

-- Priscilla Schneider

Inshallah Weave

I close my
eyes against
the heat, and
see Arabic writing

Gold script
against crimson
like a
silky carpet, deep...

My Soul-mother's
hand on
the loom, quietly
weaving promises

Borne of
the desert,
her gift of
dreams to me.

-- Priscilla Schneider

Still Life With Foghorn

Still living,
scenes of memory
collages of old days,
detailed and silent
perspective-bound by
child's recollect.

Always I return
to that house of magic
its ghost-filled rooms
tinted sepia gold
immense as remembered,
burnished by time.

And the meadow!
Then – ocean
fog veiling sand and the shore.
It's a muse
softly speaking:
I'm creating yet once more.

-- Priscilla Schneider

Storms' Solitaire

Ocean's calling,
dull roar of waves
constant on the reef;
"weather comin' our way".

Clouds are low,
The front approaches;
soft, heavy with sea-salt
seemingly touching the waves.

Ocean of many colors:
Turquoise, blue, gray, green
water tumbling
with de-light

Makes the paper
shimmer, glowing,
shining cleanly
in sunlight

And breezes caress wildly,
as I watch
and wait
and write

-- Priscilla Schneider

Wind-Baby

A white egret soars
over the valley,
wings
gleam silver,
with reflected light.

A soundless bird,
relaxing
on air currents,
a wind-baby floating
in perfect flight

And the backdrop
- a rainbow –
shimmering
over the park

Like a jewel
in the air,
it forms
a peaceful
glowing arc.

So I watch Egret,
and the Rainbow,
framing
Altona Lagoon,

Into clouds
the vision
passes; like
a dream, it fades too soon.

-- Priscilla Schneider

Peripheral Hearing

When the wind
is just right
there is a constant
dull roar; a
mumbling-rumbling
just within hearing
like a distant
plane

I look down in the
valley; maybe
it's the breeze
in the trees
now green
after all our
rain

Then, deeper sound
ocean rushing reef
off our
south shore,
its steady,
pounding rhythm
a free-flowing score

You told me once
it was the music
of the spheres,
true harmonic
convergence
inside one,
yet apart.

And I feel
blessed, to
be alive,
to have found
you – now
I listen
with my heart.

-- Priscilla Schneider

Reel Estate

I have seen
so many houses
felt the history in
each one,

The past watched
as though projected,
on my inner
screen of mind.

Like a film of
scattered images,
or like prisms in
bright light,

Like facets
-polished surfaces-
see the gemstone
of a life.

I feel the heart
-soul stories-
of the dwellers
living there.

Once I saw a
kitchen table,
settings placed as
though for guests,

Yet, just one person
-solitaire-
I saw, so quick
she left.

The poignancy
of loneliness
quiet person
quiet street

Owner of more
happy times
now quiet
in retreat.

-- Priscilla Schneider

Maroon Rain

The rains have come
sweet water, heaven's scent
we bathe, and feel
silky hair and skin,
our bodies whole again.

Warm earth blooms
flower-fragrant
with deep richness;
more rains arrive
to let us live.

Thunder masks drumbeat
lightning crackles sky
to dance our message:
--freedom!--
written from on high.

-- Priscilla Schneider

Pets

The cats care less for us than the dog,
The rooster cares the least.
They have vestiges of independence
Left over from being wild beasts.
We give them food and security;
In return we want love and fidelity.
Based on who feeds them they notice us
With no love lost, they fuss
Over whose bowl is whose.
Cats roam outside at night
And sleep on our beds by day;
The dog watches over the invalid of the house.
The cats occasionally catch a mouse;
The rooster crows to make the sun rise.
These are their gifts to share,
For us they fulfill our need to care.

-- Marge Tonks

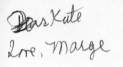

Lovers Lament

Out of his helpless condition
Comes my hopeless caregiving.
Held together by mutual consent,
Sixty-eight years of marriage contract
Ties us tightly with assent.

June thirtieth is the renewal date;
We can't make love to celebrate,
Not even a hug in a wheelchair fits
And all day long that's where he sits.

The hydraulic pump lifts him back in bed
Single, alone, with hospital rail
Restricting his moves as if being in jail.
I'm in the cot next to him, single too;
Gone is the double bed we're accustomed to.
Now we hold hands when we say goodnight
Turning away for lonely slumber
With different dreams we drift asunder.

Yesterday he asked if it was Saturday
When I replied: "Yes, our love day"
He said "But I love you every day."

-- Marge Tonks

Doggerel

Saucy's tail does its welcome wag
Her ears go up, way up to show
A friendly greeting, up they go.
Her sister, Apple, bigger than she,
Jumps up higher for me to see
She's just as smart though not as cute.
They have no speech but they're not mute
The barks are loud to express a need
It's time for drinks and time to feed.
They live inside a fenced-in yard
They know their job's to be on guard,
And warn us if a stranger's near.
They stand ready to interfere.
But dog biscuits thrown their way
Distract them from attack any day.
They woke me with barking one night,
I imagined a burglar and felt some fright.
But the intruder was a deer
I should have had nothing to fear.
The deer feels free to eat our fruits,
The dogs don't give a care,
But they'll continue to bark
As long as we have
A resident deer.

-- Marge Tonks

Nostalgia

Roland Park, Maryland, 1938-1945

When I was little, streetcars ran down streets on tracks,
brakes squealing as they approached a stop.
Close after dawn the milkman's bottles rattled
as he delivered fresh milk and picked up empties.
The iceman delivered big cakes of ice to fill
ice-box chests that stood on kitchen porches.
An organ grinder with monkey visited our street;
the monkey, dressed in red pillbox hat and jacket ,
begged for coins with a battered tin cup.
A vendor trundled his sharpening tools in a cart
along the lane behind the houses, crying:
"Bring out your knives; bring out your scissors and saws."
At noon every Saturday air-raid sirens sounded,
so promptly you could set your clocks by them.
Pied Pipers of summer, "Good Humor" trucks jingled bells
luring neighborhood children for ice cream and popsicles.
Autumn winds carried smoke laden with pungent smells
of burning brush and leaves.
Sunday evenings we gathered 'round the radio
for news of the Wars in Europe and Japan;
followed by *Jack Benny* and *The Fred Allen Show*.
On crisp winter days, freight-train whistles could be heard
wailing farewell as trains rushed on northwards.
Now more houses crowd the hills and dales.
The original players have moved on; the music of their lives
blending in the onrush of progress and new generations.

--Rosamond C. Hughes

29

Old Age

Old Age -
>Nods off while watching Television
>Awakes after midnight
>Reads for an hour or two
>Then sleeps late

Old Age -
>Measures life pill by pill
>And time by the hour
>Has difficulty matching
>Familiar faces to names

Old Age -
>Walks with care
>Finds bending down a challenge
>Struggles to rise from a comfortable chair
>Knows each joint's complaint

Old Age -
>Dislikes driving at night
>Carefully observes the roadside white line
>Finds oncoming lights blinding
>Prefers to stay at home

Old Age -
>Remembers the past fondly
>Forgets what happened yesterday
>Searches vainly for the right word
>Makes reminder lists and schedules

Old Age -
>Reads the newspaper's front page
>Checks the stock market and sports
>Then turns to the obituaries and mourns
>The passing of friends

Old Age -
>The person in the mirror
>Is not the self inside.

--Rosamond C. Hughes

Last Act

Contemporary drama,
nascent and continuous,
creating new characters.
The show must go on
but not on my stage.

So many dancers
have exited scenes
limping or leaping into shadow.
I have thoroughly
enjoyed my part.

Action slows,
lights dim,
until only a few remain.
There will be no encore.

--Rosamond C. Hughes

Earthquake

An ordinary afternoon --
Women preparing supper,
Chopping vegetables, stirring broth;
Children playing in streets;
Markets closing, workers heading home . . .
Suddenly the earth heaves,
The city shudders.
Within minutes
Buildings crumble
Streets fill with rubble:
Death, dust, devastation;
Lives forever changed or lost,
The city in ruins as
Evening falls.

--Rosamond C. Hughes

Saturday Morning Massacre

(News item: Saturday, January 8, 2011 -Safeway massacre, Tucson, Arizona, and days following)

Alienation and rage
Transform an ordinary day.
Triage and tragedy.

Shots, rapid and random;
Bewilderment.
Lives shattered.

Speculation and rumor;
Nuggets of news.
Story unspooling.

Gunman apprehended --
Unabashed, arrogant.
Reason awry.

Medical updates;
Witnesses recollect.
Media medley.

Grief, prayers, memorials;
Search for healing.
Scars remain.

Routines reestablished:
Gun Show as scheduled.

--Rosamond C. Hughes

PROSE

Patricia Gill

The Gift of Tongues

Helen Gentry, the biology professor, and I were both excited when we heard that the latest faculty member to arrive at our new college, still in its first year, was a good tennis player. The few who managed to get in early morning before-class games about three times a week would welcome such an addition.

Our excitement was short-lived, however, because within a fortnight Melly had proved to be not just a *good* player, but a near-professional, defeating everyone who challenged her to a game. Her only real competition was the pro at the Virgin Islands Hotel.

But I soon learned that she had other positive attributes. She was a wonderful person to share an office with, full of stories about her native Trinidad, her exotic family, her undergraduate and graduate years in Glasgow, where she held out for five long—and very rainy, she assured me—years without seeing her family. Her major was geography, and although she could never afford the trip home during her sojourn in Scotland, she did manage cheap student side-trips to Western Europe and could reel off the national capitals where she could find her way around like a native. She also picked up enough words in a dozen tongues to ingratiate herself wherever she went. This was in addition to flawless English and fluent French and Spanish.

Trinidad seemed small when she got back home and the job offer from the College of the Virgin Islands in St. Thomas, with its easy access to mainland America, was an offer she couldn't refuse. I soon became her devoted colleague only partially because she would cheerfully teach my Friday afternoon class in Caribbean History when I wanted to fly to New York City for the weekend to visit a wealthy friend who loved taking me to the theater.

Melly, the nickname derived from Melideana, which in turn was a corrupted form of meridian, the transposed r to l betraying the Chinese linguistic influence, enjoyed covering my class for me. These were early days in the teaching of Caribbean history and world geography; texts were hard to find and reading lists were borrowed from other disciplines. So we knew a little bit about a lot of different approaches to subjects other than our own specialties.

I noticed a change in class atmosphere after Melly had filled in for me a couple of times. When I remarked on this to my friend Helen after a tennis game she laughed and said "Well, you know, Melly really told them off when they started on the usual anti-colonialism crap."

Helen and I both suffered from covert racism,

being part of the small minority of white teachers in what was usually referred to as "a negro college." Teaching a science, Helen felt it less than I did. There was no place to hide from the facts of Caribbean history, shameful facts if your ancestors happened to be European.

"What did Melly say?" I asked, adding that it was important, obviously, for me to know if it improved my relations with the students.

"Oh, she asked them, if, even conceding the horrors of the Middle Passage, they would rather be back in a tribal village in the African bush than learning something valuable from a civilized, educated, white professor in our mongrel society. Something like that. She could say it, you know. You and I couldn't, but she could and she did."

Melly and I enjoyed our time between classes, sharing an interest in distant lands and tennis, but our developing relationship was not to last. She told me she would be leaving at the end of the semester. Again, a wonderful opportunity. A college in Kenya had offered her a full professorship at twice the salary she had been getting, with a promise of a shorter academic year and, as a professional geographer, every opportunity to travel all over the African continent. Sadly, I told her how lucky she was.

"Unfortunately, I don't know any African languages," she said. "But I guess having mastered

Mandarin I should be able to deal with the tonality of African tongues."

"You know Mandarin?" I said, surprised. She had never mentioned this before.

"Oh yes, they had a wonderful professor at the University of Glasgow. I studied it for three years. Became quite fluent. Even won an award of some sort."

Melly had won a lot of awards. But Mandarin?

"Why?" I asked. "Why did you study Mandarin?"

Melly hesitated, unusual for her, always so quick and articulate. But finally she said, slowly, "I think I told you my father's parents were Chinese."

"Well, yes, you mentioned it, but didn't say much else. I've heard about your grandfather who is part Arawak and your grandmother who is mostly French and calls you 'ma petite negre,' the one who made sure you were all duly baptized as God-fearing Episcopalians. I've heard about your two hardworking brothers who run grocery stores, but not much about the Chinese grandparents."

"Well, my father's parents came to Trinidad from China when he and my uncle were little boys. They had enough money to open one small grocery store, worked hard and now they own a chain of them. My uncle became an Episcopal priest and my brothers wanted to be businessmen, but I was the smart one, the one who did well at school. So even though I was a girl, the *only* girl in my extended family, my grandparents pampered me. My mother always said it was because I looked Chinese, with my straight hair and lighter, yellowish skin. I was definitely the favorite. I enjoyed my position of privilege, never questioned why I deserved it. Frugal as they were, my grandparents gave me everything they could, even paid my tuition at the University."

"So you wanted to repay them by learning Mandarin?"

"They never spoke Mandarin to us. They made a great effort to learn English, insisted I speak it well, rewarded me with rice candy when I learned some new esoteric word. But yes, I wanted to honor them, show my respect for their culture, they were so definitely Chinese. All that politeness and respect for family, for tradition and scholarship. At the same time I kept my Chinese studies a secret from my family so it would be a big surprise. Only my father knew since he received copies of my grades, but he didn't pay much attention. His mind was always on his sons and his business. And there was another reason."

I sensed a mystery. "Tell me," I said.

Melly sighed. "They were quiet people, my Chinese grandparents, very sedate, very dignified. Grandma especially. She was beautiful, you know, even at seventy, and as a young woman she must have been gorgeous."

"I believe it," I said. "You're pretty good looking yourself."

"Grandma was taller than I am and had a kind of quiet elegance, an air of detachment, of otherworldliness. Always in control, always graceful, except for twice a year, one day in August and again at Christmas time, when she would go completely berserk, crying and screaming things in Mandarin. She would go into the kitchen and take an old frying pan and bang, bang, bang it on the wooden table. My grandfather would stand helplessly by until she got tired of banging. When she started crying, he would take her in his arms to comfort her. The next day all went on as usual, but during Grandma's crazy spells everyone in the family would stay far away, except me. I would peek and somehow I got the idea that if I learned to talk to her in Mandarin I could help her break the spell she was under. A stupid idea. I know that now."

"No, not stupid," I said. "You had to know the truth if you were going to be able to help her."

"I should have left well enough alone, the way the others did. But no, there I was, fresh out of graduate school, PhD in hand, so proud of myself, so sure I knew more than anyone else. I remember my homecoming so well. My father and mother met me at the airport--after five years, I was so happy! We left my mother off at my eldest brother's house to help prepare the welcoming-home feast in my honor. I went into our house alone, the home we shared with my grandparents, while my father parked the car. I could hear them in the kitchen and as fate would have it, Grandma was having one of her spells--I had made a special point of getting home for Christmas."

"As I walked toward the kitchen I was so pleased with myself, so confident. I was going to prove my worth, my superior wisdom. I understood every word she was saying. But then, suddenly, I was both astounded by the clarity of my understanding and horrified by *what* she said. I turned and ran to get away, but at the front door I ran headlong into my father."

"'What is it?' he said, grasping me by the shoulders to restrain my flight."

"Oh Pappy," I said. "Is it true?"

"My father led me to a chair. We could hear my grandmother sobbing in the kitchen, which meant the tantrum was nearing its end."

"If you mean about selling my sister for money enough to get the family to America, yes, it's true. My father took care of the sale, but the decision was my mother's, to sell her daughter to save her sons. She has never forgiven herself. But," my father added slowly and carefully, "she never wanted you children to know. She wanted no one to share in her anguish. Even in her madness, she spoke only Mandarin. It never occurred to her that any of you might understand."

"My father said that my grandmother was afraid we might all feel as guilty as she did," Melly told me as I sat there unable to speak. "And she worried about retribution, that it might all be transitory--the wealth the family had acquired, the success of her grandsons, the achievements of her talented granddaughter, me, her favorite, it was so undeserved, so tainted. Everything we had came from the enslavement of her daughter. Every year on her daughter's birthday and the anniversary of her sale, my grandmother cursed herself and asked God to forgive us all."

"She never knew," Melly said. "Neither my father nor I ever told her. I guarded her secret and kept my own. I never mentioned my ability to understand and speak Mandarin to anyone until now. It wasn't such a gift, after all, was it? The ability to speak in many tongues."

--Patricia Gill

Caregiver

Being a caregiver is rewarding no matter how much energy it requires. I started caregiving when Interfaith Coalition of Saint Croix began their program in 1995. I took their training course for volunteers and have stayed with it for 16 years of community service. To me caregiving includes taking care of myself and taking care of others.

My first assignment was to make a weekly visit to Raphael, an elderly man who had just retired from a long-time position as a pastry chef at the Buccaneer Hotel. He had lost his driver's license when he put his foot on the accelerator instead of the brake and crashed into a building in a shopping mall. Grateful that he didn't hit a person and was not hurt himself, he regretted he could not drive to do the shopping. His wife still worked, leaving him home alone with nothing he could do for her.

Raphael had proposed to his wife when she was in her twenties and he was in his fifties. He did not tell her his age. He had retired in his nineties, and she was in her sixties and still working.

He was charming, a talented song composer and artist, an appealing person to have as a friend. My husband and I took him out for breakfast every Saturday during the three years before he died. One Saturday when he was ninety-seven he said he thought he was getting old. He had difficulty going up and down the steep steps to his house. He told his son he wanted to visit Guatemala, his birth place, once more. To his delight his son took him there. It was his last trip.

When he was dying in the hospital, I was able to hold his hand even though he no longer recognized me. I missed him very much when he was gone. I was blessed to have known him.

My second assignment was to take Isabel Mason out every Tuesday. She was in her nineties, diagnosed with incurable cancer and losing her sight. She was determined to continue managing her life with whatever help she needed to cope with her necessities. She asked for a housekeeper, a bookkeeper, and healthcare from Continuum Care. This team followed her instructions.

Isabel had Tuesdays well planned in advance. No matter how awful she felt, she wanted to go with me as I did her errands. These included mail, banking, food, supplies, prescriptions, cameras, miscellaneous. She had frequent appointments with doctors and her favorite dentist. It was a heavy workout starting at 10a.m. and ending at 4p.m. We always had lunch at Wendy's - Five dollars for two of us. She was a millionaire penny pincher.

Isabel's life story needs to be written. It would read like a novel. She was born and raised in London, survived the German bombing during World War II, she started journaling while she was working for the Red Cross. Her leather bound journals are now in the hands of a writer who will use them to write her saga. I would like to read them in order to understand Isabel better. She hardly knew the word "love." Her key word was "control." She ordered me to "demand to see Dan, the pharmacist I depend on." "I don't demand, I ask kindly." I replied. "You have to *demand* to get what you want," she insisted.

She never understood that her attitude lost friends faster than she could make new ones. I surmised that she hadn't had much experience with love. She was divorced and had no children. She did love her two cats.

When she left England to seek her fame and fortune in New York, she found fame as a concert pianist, composer and piano teacher but not the fortune. Coming to Saint Croix where music teachers are not wealthy, she made a bundle in the real estate business.

In her will she left her Steinway grand piano to the Juilliard School with funds to ship it to New York. She left her house and car to the man who did her financial work every Sunday with no pay. She left me a thousand times more than that in my memory of her.

When I went to Maine for a summer visit, she resented my absence as her caregiver. She threatened that she would not be alive when I returned. I called her from Maine to say what day I would return and she sounded very much alive. I flew in late Sunday night, August 11th. When I called her the next morning there was no answer. Always in control, she kept her word and had died just as my plane touched down on Saint Croix. I miss her very much. She had my love without knowing what it was.

My third assignment was to do errands and be a friend to Marta who had incurable cancer. I had been trained to be a counselor to patients who were dying but Marta didn't want to think about death.

"I am not dying of cancer," she said, "I am living with cancer."

She was unwilling to use what I could offer spiritually. She did need help with errands, mostly getting medications. Friends brought her food.

When she ended up in the hospital I was with her when she took her last breath. Before I had a chance to call the nurse two friends came to visit. I didn't tell them she had died as I had heard that the ears are the last to go and maybe she would hear the lovely Spanish words from her friends as they said their farewells. After they left, I called the nurse who verified Marta had departed. She was still young and had no relatives on Saint Croix. It was sad.

My next assignment was to go on Thursdays to relieve the fulltime housekeeper who took care of Aster, an Alzheimer patient. Aster's husband interviewed me before entrusting her to my care. He was living in a hospice in New York and had been warned that his life would soon be ending. He did die less than a year later leaving his wife bereaved. Even though she had no memory of anything else, she knew he was gone.

Aster didn't remember me from week to week. Every Thursday she greeted me: "Who are you? What is your name? Who sent you? Why are you here? How did you know about me?"

She was particularly interested in who sent me. She asked questions about Interfaith over and over again. Her housekeeper spoke only Spanish but Aster was bilingual. This was my chance to learn Spanish. She loaned me a textbook. We did a lesson every week. She assigned homework but didn't remember what lesson we were on. Consequently she couldn't scold me when I asked to do a lesson we had already completed but I hadn't done the homework. She was a sweet, lovable woman. I was her caregiver for about three years.

There were two other women assigned to me for a short time as they needed to live with family rather than alone. There is no private residential facility on Saint Croix for those who need constant care.

My longest and most unhappy caregiving was for my husband who had Parkinson's disease and could no longer walk. For three years I fed him, moved him from bed to wheelchair and back, provided entertainment and listened, broken hearted, to him talk of his desire to walk again.

Gradually he grew weaker. He could only read one page, didn't understand the movie, ate only half his dinner, took one sip of his rum, and slept a lot. One evening a month before his ninety-seventh birthday, he stopped breathing. By his bedside were the three women who loved him but couldn't save him. I miss him terribly.

I asked for some time off before a new assignment. When I was ready I was introduced to Claudette who was blind. I didn't tell her that my first four receivers all died.

When she called me this week to ask me to take her to WAPA, she asked me to come at two o'clock. She knows the time as she has a talking clock. I beeped my horn to let her know I had arrived; she tapped her cane along the path from her house to the gate, unlocked the gate and felt her way to my car. We picked up her mail from the box near her house, paid the electric bill, went shopping at Plaza Extra (she had a memorized list) and returned home to unload the heavy bags.

I was home by four thirty, exhausted from the two-hour stint. Claudette managed her disability magnificently. She was in her seventies and had been blind for ten years. We became good friends. She passed away from diabetes.

This year I celebrate my ninety fifth birthday. I may have to be switched from the Caregiver's List to the Care Receiver's Program. Elisa McKay will know when to do that, she manages the program with attention to details and with sustaining love for all of us.

-- Marge Tonks

Alone

Alone for the first time in my life after sixty-nine years of marriage, I contemplate my new freedom. My family and close friends have kindly accepted my joy when they may have expected grief. No mourning now compared to the last three years of deep sadness as I watched my invalid husband fade away. Parkinson's disease had taken its toll. He yearned to walk again in spite of the medical verdict that he couldn't. His misery was only slightly contagious as I struggled to maintain my own inner peace along with our shared sadness. It was a long, strenuous stretch of years that finally ended painlessly and peacefully for him when his body died.

My release from responsibility gave me a lift. I miss him. I love him, but now am free to start anew to create my own style of living and explore who I am without a partner. He said he thought the worst thing that might happen to a human being would be to lose a spouse. I am glad he didn't have to do it. I am grateful that I am alone.

Being alone does not make me lonely. I have a daughter, two sons, two dogs, two cats, two roosters, two hens, friendly neighbors, caring friends, and belong to two churches and two groups I see on Mondays and Thursdays.

It is in my bedroom that I am alone. Decorating a room of my own had first priority after my husband's burial at sea and the memorial service. Our daughter Marilyn, who lives in an apartment in our house, is always there for me when I need her. But I cherish the independence of my own space.

Our sons came for the ceremonials and help me with the business matters. I asked them to take everything belonging to their dad out of our room. It was a week-long task to convert the room. Closets and drawers were emptied as well as bookshelves and files. When they had disposed of everything, they moved furniture to convert the room, and my daughter-in-law painted one wall a warm lime color and we hung my favorite pictures and photos on it.

The head of my single bed faces east. I watch the sunrise without getting up. The roosters wake me before sunrise. I don't have to consult a clock to know it is morning. I say good morning to my beloved husband who doesn't answer because he doesn't believe there is life after death. I greet him anyway in case he has discovered that his spirit still lives. After my sons left to return to their own homes, I not only enjoyed my new single bedroom, I also adjusted to meals alone. There is no one waiting in his hospital bed for me to feed him from his breakfast tray and ready him for the hospice nurse that came to bathe him. Before she left she would settle him in his wheelchair with his medications, radio and book.

When I went out on necessary errands, I was constantly aware that he was home alone with dogs, cats and poultry but no human help if he needed it. It was with a sigh of relief when I returned to find him still in his chair, lonely and tired, ready to go back to bed again.

Three times he fell asleep in the afternoon and didn't awake until the next morning. I slept lightly, listening to hear whether he was breathing. In the morning I was so relieved that he was still alive. I wanted him to stay alive as long as he wanted. I watched him grow weaker with less interest in his surroundings. He would sit with a book opened to the same page for an hour. He began to eat less and not drink his daily rum; at dinner he would watch CNN. I fed him as he sat in front of the TV. Now I have blessed silence while eating my veggie dinner by myself, not knowing how many were killed in Iraq or Afghanistan. The TV isn't totally neglected. After "Jeopardy" there comes the best moment of relief when I no longer have to pump the lifting machine to move him from his wheelchair to his bed.

One night I broke down and sobbed, "I'm tired of this." My precious, helpless, mate said he was sorry. We wept together. I don't weep now.

As his goal to live to be one hundred faded away, I reminded him of his past pleasures, accomplishments, and awards for excellent performances. He looked at photos of his boats from the first barrel boat he built to the beautiful Choy Lee ketch he sailed to the Galapagos in the Pacific and to the Mediterranean across the Atlantic.

Reviewing his life with him was contrary to my own desire to live in only the present. I like to put the past in a storage bin, let the future happen as it may, and live fully in the NOW. But I must admit that looking at old photos was fun. I have a deep drawer full of photos waiting to go into albums that will entice me now that I have time to do it.

While we were reliving some past experiences together it was interesting to hear him remember his childhood but not all of his adulthood. This is a common human loss of short term memory while retaining memories of long ago events. This has already happened for me: I don't know where I put something an hour ago but I know where I was ten years ago, or even fifteen years ago.

I have to make a schedule every day to remember what my plan for the day is. At night I read my plan of the day to see how much of it worked. Then I tear it up and forget it until I start over the next day. I trust my memory to recall three things but when there are more I have to make a written list and remember to look at it.

Celebrating my freedom includes listening to Rachmaninoff instead of Beethoven, eating broccoli and cucumbers which my husband never liked, reading in bed, going to lunch or dinner with friends, going to concerts and the theatre, and soon to start traveling again. I am determined to learn to live alone happily and not be bogged down by memories. Morning meditations center me; daily spiritual readings support me; swimming, walking, and eating vegetarian keep me healthy. Above all, my friends are more than "just a phone call away." They respond to my need to be with them and respect my times alone. I feel no self-pity. I know how solid our marriage was. I declare contentment being alone without loneliness. I loved my partner before and during his illness and now I love him for what he taught me during his final years.

-- Marge Tonks

A Tropical Murder Case

Sherlock Holmes strode into our rooms at 221B Baker Street, shaking sleet and snow from his coat. He pulled off the coat, shook it out and hung it on the hall tree. It was January, and outside, the wind howled and hurled sleet onto the freezing residents brave enough to face the weather. It was the worst winter I could recall.

"Ready for a vacation in the tropics, Watson?" he asked, smiling.

"Any time, Holmes. Perhaps a trip to the moon?"

"I am not joking, my friend. I have just come from the Danish Embassy. They have engaged us, yes, you too, to investigate the death of the Lieutenant Governor of the Danish West Indies. His body was found on the island where he presided, St. Croix in the Virgin Islands. The local police are unequipped to look into the matter, and as the victim was a personal friend of His Majesty, no expense will be spared. Let us pack our summer wear and tomorrow we will take train to Southampton where will board a ship to our destination. I understand that St. Croix has a most salubrious climate."

The next morning, we hired a four-wheeler and slipped and slid to Victoria Station. I felt pity for the poor horses bearing the brunt of the freezing weather. A few were covered with a blanket, but most were not. The train was well-heated, however, and by the time we reached the seaport, the rain and sleet had stopped. We were able to board our ship, a Danish passenger and freight carrier and make ourselves comfortable in our cabin.

The next day, the ship sailed into rough seas, but by the time we reached the Madeiras, our first stop, the skies had turned blue and the temperature had climbed to a comfortable sixty-five degrees. At the suggestion of the captain, we visited the wine shop of Blandy's, a respected purveyor of the famous Madeira wines. We were invited to sample several versions and arranged for a case for each of us to be delivered to our ship. We were able to spend a day visiting the island and then reboarded for the second leg of our Argosy.

My experience with ocean travel had been limited to military transport, so it was with pleasure that I was able to enjoy the comforts and dining experience of a passenger ship.

Holmes had been given a thick portfolio on the Virgin Islands and we both studied it in the comfort of the ship. We learned that the islands had been governed by Spain, England, Holland, The Knights of Malta and France before being taken over by Denmark, some century and a half ago. Originally, slaves were imported to work the sugar fields, but they had been freed in 1848. Their economic condition did not improve, however, and an uprising in St. Croix, termed "The Fireburn" had destroyed many plantations and the town of Frederiksted. St. Thomas no longer raised sugar cane, but its magnificent harbour made it a natural coaling port and free-trade facility. St. Croix, the larger of the islands, still raised cane, but the world market had deteriorated due to the availability of the cheaper beet sugar.

We reached St. Thomas in the Danish Virgin Islands, and were met by an official of the government. He explained that St. Croix had no harbor deep enough for our ship, so we would be boarded on an inter-island steam launch for the final leg. A dozen other passengers joined us on the launch, including one rather rough-looking man who kept very much to himself. The trip took four hours, across a blue sea, with gentle trade winds caressing us. We threaded the reefs into Christiansted harbour and landed at a wharf next to the fort. There we were met by a young man who introduced himself as the private secretary to the late Lieutenant Governor.

"My name is Nils Jorgensen," he said, "I will have your bags taken up to the hotel while I acquaint you with the situation."

"I am surprised that everyone we've met here speaks English," Holmes remarked, "I expected nothing but Danish."

Jorgensen chuckled. "Official correspondence is in Danish, but these islands have adopted American English since the beginning, as we are much closer to America than Europe. Let us go to my office in Government House."

We remarked on the clean and handsome shops along the street, and noted that negroes vastly outnumbered white persons. Behind us, at the waterfront, labourers were rolling barrels onto an island trading vessel. "Those casks hold rum," Jorgensen explained. "Despite the drop in sugar revenue, the rum made from molasses more than makes up for it."

In Jorgensen's office, we gathered around a table on which a map of the island was laid out. "Here is where Governor Knudsen was found, at the shoreline near the Salt River. You see that the entire island is laid out in plots of about 150 acres or so, and named by the proprietors as they chose, often after their daughters, such as Anna's Hope, Mary's Fancy, or some other fancy."

"What do these symbols represent?" asked Holmes, pointing to marks on some of the plots.

"They indicate working sugar mills. There are not many left these days."

"I would like to go out tomorrow to see

where Knudsen was found. I note that there is a mill there. Perhaps we could see that as well. You could explain that we are visiting from England and are just curious. I would like not to have our real mission disclosed as of yet," Holmes asked.

"Of course. By the way, Governor Knudsen could claim ancestry all the way back to King Canute, with whom you English are acquainted."

Jorgensen walked with us to our hotel, actually the only one in the town, a large new building a few hundred yards away. We were introduced to the proprietor and his wife, Captain and Mrs. Pentheny, and escorted to our rooms. Our bags had been unpacked and we washed and changed from our travel stained garments into more comfortable wear.

Upon descending to the lobby, we were greeted by a waiter bearing two tall frosted glasses. "Enjoy our island rum punch," Mrs. Pentheny smiled, "We will serve dinner in the courtyard in about an hour."

The punch was followed by another and we then retired to a table in the courtyard, illuminated by paper lanterns. The menu offered a variety of island foods: curried lamb, local fish, conch and lobster. Our choice of a lobster starter was presented in a lightly spiced sauce and the curried lamb was as good as any to be had in London.

Captain Pentheny appeared and said, "May I join you? It is not often that we have such distinguished visitors to our island."

"With pleasure," Holmes replied, "I hope you will not mind if I question you about the late Lieutenant Governor."

"Please ask. I shall be glad to help in any way. It was a shock to us to have our leader killed."

"Tell me, Captain Pentheny, what kind of man was the governor? Was he well-liked? Did anyone have a particular antipathy toward him?" Holmes asked.

"Governor Knutsen was not an easy man to know," Pentheny replied, "He tended to be stiff and formal. His family plantation was destroyed during the rebellion and he never forgave those who were responsible. He carried a grudge against the coloured workers, and his dislike was returned with interest. They remembered that he led the volunteer company that protected Christiansted with guns, where several were killed."

"Would anyone have carried that feeling to the point where he might have been at risk, even though twenty-five years have passed?"

"Revenge is a dish best served cold," I remarked.

"I doubt that, although one cannot be sure," Pentheny mused. "As chief magistrate, he tended to impose harsh sentences on the workers."

I looked up at the brilliant stars above us. "Look, Holmes, what a clear sky. No fog or haze here!"

"I shall have to see if I can drag this case out until at least the month of May," Holmes joked, "But for now, I am ready to retire. It has been a long and eventful day."

Next morning, we met Jorgensen and reviewed Knutsen's schedule. He had been in the habit of riding out each morning for the past two weeks to various plantations. "Did he have an escort with him?" Holmes asked.

"Normally, yes, but that morning, the entire corporal's guard reported sick."

"That is most suspicious," Holmes commented, "Can you arrange for me to interview the garrison surgeon later?"

Jorgensen brought around a trap and we jogged out to the place at Salt River where the body was found. Holmes looked about and made note of various objects there: bits of broken glass, a piece of a broken iron gear wheel, pieces of rope and clumps of coarse grass.

"What happened to the governor's horse?"

"It was nearby. It's reins had caught on some branches and it was patiently waiting to be freed," Jorgensen answered.

Not far away, we saw a tall smokestack alongside a conical stone structure, obviously the mill. A smaller cone stood a few yards away. As we walked toward the mill, a man came out of a large house nearby. I was startled to see that he had been our fellow passenger on the launch. Holmes gripped my arm to warn me not to notice that we had met before.

"My friends here from England are curious about the operation of a sugar mill. Perhaps you can explain?"

Reilly gestured toward the mill. "It's what you see. The steam engine is supplied with steam from the boiler and stack, burning bagasse, the cane stalks, or coal if necessary. Those iron rollers crush the cane, and the juice is led down to boiling pans to reduce the liquid to a syrup. It is then taken elsewhere to be refined further and converted to sugar."

"And what is that structure?" Holmes asked, pointing to the other, smaller cone.

"Oh, that is only a well and windmill pump. It is unsafe to enter it as the stonework is crumbling. Now, I must get back to work. These fellows will stop if you take your eyes off them for a minute."

Reilly headed off and Jorgensen whispered, "There is little cane grown here now. The mill is rented out to other growers in season. Down there is where the Governor was found." He gestured to the water's edge, not far away.

We pushed our way through some small brush and Holmes stooped and picked something up which he put in his pocket. "What did the examination of Knudsen's body show to be the cause of death?"

"He was killed by a blow to the back of the head. It is possible he was thrown from his horse and struck a stone, but the surgeon claims that is unlikely."

"I wonder if that cudgel Reilly carries matches the blow," Holmes mused. "Is there any way you can arrange for Reilly to be held in custody without associating him with the murder? I especially wish to examine the club."

"That won't be a problem," Jorgensen chuckled, "Today is Friday and Reilly can be depended upon to come into town, get drunk and cause trouble. I'll have him arrested and jailed for drunk and disorderly. We have more powers here than you have in London."

We arrived at the spot where Knudsen's body had been discovered. We learned that his clothes were found to be dirty and with bits of grass and twigs caught in it. It took no great stretch to assume that he had been killed elsewhere and dragged there.

We returned to town and Holmes found the apothecary where he purchased certain reagents. Holmes was not surprised to find that the button he had found and pocketed matched the coat the Governor had been wearing when he was found. We spent the rest of the day examining the Governor's appointment book. It appeared that for the week previous to his death, he had taken his horse and ridden out into the countryside. Each day, he visited a different plantation, each having a mill. It appeared he had been looking for something, and possibly it had found him instead. Jorgensen promised to look for Knudsen's private letter file for clues.

When we interviewed the garrison surgeon, he assured us that there was nothing sinister in the entire guard being ill.

"On the night before, they all went to Mama Mary's for dinner. That is a little hole-in-the-wall in Freetown, just a few blocks away. She served them all a conch stew but neglected to tell them that the conch had been bought the day before, and without ice, had spoiled. Next day, every one was doubled up with diarrhea and vomiting. She had heavily seasoned the stew to cover the taste. Later that week, the men visited her and destroyed her kitchen. All in good fun."

That disposed of the conspiracy theory.

We dined well and slept well that night and next morning, learned that Reilly was, indeed, incarcerated. Holmes examined the club that Reilly had been carrying and found, not to anyone's surprise, that it was bloodstained, faintly, but positively. The charge against Reilly was raised to 'suspicion of murder', and we returned to Judith's Fancy.

"I wondered why Reilly was so anxious about keeping us away from the well," Holmes remarked, "I noticed it had a padlock on the door."

The lock was no problem for Holmes' skill and picklocks and we stepped inside. There was the pump casing with a rod extending to the crank at the top. The well itself was about four feet across and seemed to be in excellent condition. A windlass was mounted above it, and secured to the end of the windlass rope was a plank, like a bos'ns chair. Holmes shone a bull's eye lantern down into the well but could see nothing useful.

"Gentlemen I propose going down into the well. The rope seems to be new and strong. If you will lower me down and pull me back up, I would be obliged."

He stripped to his drawers and settled into the chair. We cranked him up and then down into the well, a distance of perhaps fifty feet. We heard a splash when his feet struck the water and then silence. "There is something here, under the water," he called, "See if you can find a pole with a hook."

There was, indeed such a pole and we lowered it to him. We heard a bit of splashing and then a cry of triumph. "Pull me up, fellows!"

We cranked up the windlass and Holmes held out an object in his hand. He disengaged himself from the chair and presented his prize. "A silver tea pot, by God. And there are more things there. Jorgensen, can you find a diver, someone who can go down and recover all that is in the well?"

"Not a problem, Mr. Holmes. We have men here who dive for conch and lobster. For a few Kroner, I can find an honest man. But what do you make of the teapot?"

"It is the reason Reilly murdered Governor Knudsen. This trove is probably from the Fireburn. Plantation owners whose places were threatened bundled up their valuables and sank them in wells outside the trouble areas. I will wager you will find that they were originally in a sack or net so they could be retrieved. Chances are, Knudsen was asked by descendants of the owners to try to locate the goods. Obviously, Reilly had discovered them and was selling them one piece at a time in St. Thomas. When Knudsen came across this well, Reilly panicked and killed him. He probably planned to sink his body in the deep water offshore where it would never be found."

A diver recovered not only many silver items, but a jar full of gold pieces. A letter in Governor Knudsen's file confirmed that he was asked to locate the hoard, long thought to have been lost to rioters.

Gallows Bay reaffirmed its designation when Reilly was hanged there, but after two wonderful weeks we had already left for home and winter, bearing a letter of appreciation from Governor Hansen and the thanks of Jorgensen.

-- Alvin Rymsha

Rosamond Hughes

Invisible Friend

"Mrs. Thompson, this is Mrs. Blackburn at school. I need to talk to you about Teddy. Do you have some time today that you could spare before you pick him up?" Her voice was full of concern. Jean held the phone while trying to quiet her dog which was barking loudly. Mrs. Blackburn was Principal of Saint Jude's Academy which Teddy had been attending since he was three.

"Yes, of course. Is there anything wrong?"

"Teddy is fine and is with our counselor, Mrs. Jackson, but his teacher says that his behavior is becoming more and more disruptive. We've spoken of this before. Meet me at two p.m. You know where my office is. Mrs. Jackson and his teacher, Miss Packard, will be joining us soon."

Jean hung up the receiver; the dog, who had been dancing around just out of reach, stopped barking.

"One of these days, Bowser, if you don't stop this nonsense it's back to the Pound with you." She wondered if dogs had psychic powers as

Bowser only barked when a call involved Teddy of whom he was very protective.

Jean worried about Teddy who was six years old and very active. Many little kids have 'invisible friends' who eventually are forgotten but Teddy was different. Ever since he could talk, he was content to play by himself as if there was another child with whom he held long conversations in a language he made up. He called the invisible sharer Mikey. Mikey sometimes 'answered' through Teddy in a distinctly different voice, loud and petulant. As Teddy grew older and was occasionally naughty he would claim: "Mikey made me do it." Dr. Bagley, their pediatrician, had assured Jean that it was only a phase and would go away after Teddy became more socialized with other children. Jean organized play groups and was surprised to find the other children seemed to accept Mikey and even learned 'Mikey talk.' They thought it funny when Mikey answered them and wanted to know if they might have a secret friend too. It became a concern and an embarrassment but she trusted Dr. Bagley. She'd passed the information on to the nursery school and kindergarten teachers, but Mikey did not go away, in fact he seemed to grow with Teddy. Teddy's father, Lloyd, referred to him as 'Mischievous Mikey.' Teddy was a gentle child, but Mikey was obstreperous and became more so as Teddy grew older.

Teddy was an unusual looking little boy. He was small for his age with an oddly shaped head that seemed too big for his body. He could not remember a time when Mikey had not been with him. They did everything together. Sometimes Mikey talked through Teddy, and sometimes they held conversations in the comfortable privacy of Teddy's mind. Teddy didn't consider Mikey invisible in the same way his mother did; Mikey was just there the same way as his hands and feet.

As Teddy grew, Mikey grew, but Mikey was distinctly different and sometimes bullied Teddy, and became angry because he wasn't 'free.' He relied on Teddy for everything. In frustration he would complain: "*If only I had my own body...*"

The real trouble began when Teddy was five years old and entered the kindergarten at Saint Jude's Academy, a school that specialized in teaching children with learning challenges: children who were ADHA, borderline autistic, or who had other learning difficulties. Teddy was an exceptional case because he was very bright and didn't fit any of the categories, but his invisible friend was a problem.

As the months went by it became harder to control Mikey, particularly when the children learned they could goad Teddy into throwing a tantrum. One boy, Jackie O'Malley, particularly upset him. Jackie was a natural bully who loved to boss and ridicule his classmates. He was built like a bulldog, low, muscular, and meaty.

"Invisible friends are for babies," Jackie jeered. "You're a baby - baby, baby, baby."

"*Kick him, Teddy,*" Mikey commanded, "*Make him stop laughing at me. Kick him, kick him.*"

Teddy would try to calm Mikey.

"Mikey, you gotta stop being naughty," he'd plead, "It gets us in trouble."

"*I'm not naughty, you're naughty.   Besides, they don 't like me.*"

"Then be quiet, just talk to me within."

"*That's no fun.   Then nobody knows I'm here.*"

"I do, I always do."

Jean parked her car near the school and walked the short distance to the main entrance. There was a hint of spring in the air, the ground was soft and the trees were budding. She hummed as she walked up the steps to the school. Mrs. Blackburn, a short, round, middle-aged woman with a friendly manner, greeted her in the front hall.

"Mrs. Thompson, I'm so glad you could come today. Please follow me."

They walked down a corridor and into a pleasant office with a large desk, some full sized chairs, some child-sized chairs, and a low table covered with toys and cards.

"Please have a seat and make yourself comfortable; as you can see, my office is sometimes used as a testing room. Mrs. Jackson and Miss Packard will be here shortly. Sally Earnshaw, the teaching assistant, is taking the class. Mrs. Jackson sent Teddy back to class after working with him this morning."

"Is Teddy alright? Has he been acting up?"

"Teddy is fine but is becoming increasingly disruptive. He is very bright and learns quickly; in fact he is way ahead of the others and often tries to help them. It's this invisible 'Mikey' friend that is our problem."

Jean groaned, "I don't know how to deal with 'Mikey'. Dr. Bagley assured me that it was only a matter of time; many young children have 'invisible friends' but they outgrow them."

The door opened and in came Miss Packard, a young energetic blonde not many years out of college, accompanied by Mrs. Jackson, a tall primly dressed woman with grey hair, a sharp pointed nose, and gold-rimmed glasses that enlarged her near-sighted blue eyes.

"Hi, Mrs. Thompson, how are you?" Miss Packard said, seating herself with nimble grace on one of the child-sized chairs. Mrs. Jackson chose the remaining adult chair, settling into it slowly.

"Thank you both for coming." Mrs. Blackburn began. "We are all concerned for Teddy who has lots of potential but, as you know, has some behavioral problems. Please tell Mrs. Thompson what happened today, Miss Packard."

"First of all, I'd like to say that Teddy is generally a pleasure to teach and can be very helpful. He is quick, bright, and eager to learn."

"I'm glad you find him so, he really enjoys

your class." Jean remarked.

"There have been incidents before this, but minor ones. Teddy sometimes has trouble dealing with other children, some of whom are slow and unfocused. Rather 'Mikey' has trouble with them. Teddy is a gentle child and seems to be willing to help others but his other persona is mean, impatient, and provocative. Teddy seems unaware or cannot control this invisible friend that sometimes seems to speak through him. What might have been ignored or found amusing in Kindergarten has become a real problem in First Grade. Yesterday he hit another child and called him dumb and lazy in a most unpleasant voice. When I tried to calm him he seemed to understand but said 'That's Mikey, he's naughty.' But then his voice changed and he swore and began to shout in gibberish. I tried to quiet him but decided to send him to Mrs. Jackson to see if she could help him. This morning he was fine for the first hour but then started misbehaving and shouting in gibberish. I had to remove him again and take him to Mrs. Jackson."

"He was not at all cooperative." Mrs. Jackson said. "At first he seemed to be trying, but when I tried to draw him out about his 'imaginary' friend, his voice changed and he began using words no normal six-year old uses, and threw a tantrum.

He's never done that before. When he calmed down, his voice became normal and he began to cry. I've tested Teddy; he is not an ADHD child except when his 'invisible friend' takes over. Recently he has had trouble controlling this fantasy."

Mrs. Blackburn broke in: "As you know Mrs. Thompson, this school specializes in working with children with learning difficulties, but this one is most unusual. We can't have this behavior in the classroom. May I suggest that you withdraw him from school for a few weeks and have him tested? Mrs. Jackson suggests that Dr. Sybil Magee at University Hospital would be willing to see him. She's a pediatric psychiatrist who specializes in behavioral disorders."

"I took the liberty of asking her if she might consider accepting him in a study she is doing and she was very interested. She has had good results and appreciates the difficulties the families and children have." Mrs. Jackson peered at Jean through her thick-lensed glasses. Jean felt as if her depths were being plumbed for hidden clues.

Mrs. Jackson continued; "I don't think Teddy is schizophrenic. If 'Mikey' can be banished, I'm sure he would be relieved and become a normal little boy."

She handed Jean a card with Dr. Magee's office number. Jean looked down at the floor wondering what she should do; she really wanted to talk with her husband and Dr. Bagley before making a decision.

"Give me a little time to think about this. Of course we want what is best for Teddy; he's our only child and he has struggled with his 'secret sharer' almost since birth. We kept hoping he would outgrow it but it's getting stronger. It's as if he's possessed, but we don't believe in that sort of thing. As a matter of fact, I was planning to make an appointment with Dr. Bagley."

There was never a time in Teddy's short life that he had been alone. The other, the one whom he came to call Mikey, had always been there inside his head. Together they came into the world and became aware of its astonishing complexities. From the beginning they were in close communication; what Teddy felt, Mikey felt, and what Teddy saw or heard Mikey also did. When Teddy first learned to talk he babbled as if he was talking to someone else and they were talking to him, which, of course, was exactly what was happening. Mikey and Teddy developed their own language and Teddy had to learn English as his second language, but his parents didn't understand this.

Teddy could spend hours playing alone, coloring, building with blocks, playing with trucks and cars, always babbling in a strange language. Occasionally there would be a disagreement and it would appear that Teddy was having a fit or tantrum. He'd even hit himself.

Mikey, his invisible friend, was often destructive and frustrated. Jean thought it was merely Teddy's excuse for inappropriate behavior.

"Build a house, build a house; I don't want to play dumb old cars..."

"No, Mikey, I've already arranged cars in a circle..."

"You never let me do anything I want, Teddy."

"But we agreed to play cars and trucks."

"No we didn't, I don't want to..."

There would be kicking and screaming and throwing toys. Jean would have to step in and put a stop to it. To her the talk sounded like gobbling. She thought he was playing with his invisible friend whom she had come to accept as a childhood aberration.

"Stop it Teddy, stop it right now. Calm down. Let's draw some pictures or color." Eventually he would calm down and stop crying.

One morning he overheard his mother talking to Dr. Bagley on the telephone phone.

"I really think you should see him, Dr. Bagley. It's getting worse and he is acting out at school. They've asked me to keep him home for a few weeks and take him to Dr. Magee for some testing and therapy."

"Now see what you've done, Mikey, we'll have to go see old Baggie again." Teddy grumbled

"*I don't care. You see him. I'm going to hide.*"

Dr. Bagley was their pediatrician but he specialized in treating children that had special challenges. He had been observing Teddy since the age of three when Mikey became a 'problem,' not just a make-believe invisible playmate.

From their first meeting, Teddy had been friendly and cooperative, but Mikey became increasingly belligerent. Sometimes Teddy spoke for Mikey; sometimes Mikey spoke directly through Teddy as if he had taken him over. Though Dr. Bagley consulted with Jean, he preferred that she did not stay in the room for these sessions.

Today Teddy overheard Dr. Bagley discussing his case with his mother. Teddy had not been interested, but Mikey was indignant.

"What are they talking about?" Mikey had said, *"I don't have any problems. It's you, Teddy/'*

"You're my problem, Mikey. You make me do bad things that get us in trouble."

"No I don't" Mikey objected *"I just want to have fun; I want to be as free as you are only I don't know how."*

"Stop talking to yourself, Teddy." Jean said as she pushed him ahead into Dr. Bagley's office. As usual, she took a seat in the waiting room and he went into the playroom.

"Well, well, Teddy, how are you today?" the good doctor began.

"Okay" Teddy answered cautiously, going over to the toy table to sit down. He knew the routine.

"And how is Mikey?"

"He's hiding."

"Why is he hiding?"

Teddy picked up a red block and stacked it on a blue one before answering.

"He doesn't like you. He doesn't want to speak to you?"

"Did he tell you why he doesn't want to speak to me?"

"He says he doesn't have any problems and you're too nosey and ask too many questions."

"How do you feel about that?

"Well, I didn't want to come either, but you're okay." The doctor went on talking, but Teddy wasn't listening. *"Tell him blocks are boring."* Mikey was back.

"Tell him yourself." Teddy replied.

"Mikey is back?" the doctor asked.

"Yes, but I don't want to bother with him. I want to go home."

Dr. Bagley kept talking and showing him pictures, hoping to lure Mikey into conversation. But Mikey was making so much noise in Teddy's head that he couldn't pay attention. Finally the session was over. Dr. Bagley agreed that Dr. Magee might be worth consulting.

"She's doing some remarkable work at University Hospital."

At last they were on their way home. Teddy's head ached badly; it always did after he and Mikey fought, only it seemed to be getting worse.

"Why didn't you answer Dr. Bagley? He's trying to help you."

"Mikey was making too much noise and wouldn't talk to Bags."

"Dr. Bagley, Teddy. Don't be rude. He's a kind man...."

Mikey broke in, "*I don't need any help. There's nothing wrong with me except I can't get out.*"

He spoke clearly through Teddy but in a different tone, rougher and louder. Jean had become aware of this when Teddy was younger and had played along with Mikey until she realized that Teddy was not playing games with her.

"Mikey try to help Teddy. You are

making a lot of trouble for him by not behaving. Be his friend."

Mikey didn't answer; in fact they drove the rest of the way home in silence.

"Can we go to the park after lunch, Mom? Can I ride my bike?" Teddy asked as they turned into the driveway and pulled into the garage,

"We'll see. I'll call Betty Wells; maybe she can join us and bring Billy."

"Billy's such a slowpoke. He never wants to do anything fun."

"Behave yourself, Mikey. It's a wonder you have any friends."

"I like Billy," Teddy said. "Mikey does, too; he's just in a bad mood."

"Am not!" Mikey muttered.

Teddy dropped his coat on the hall bench and ran into the living room to his special corner with the brightly painted bookcase and toy box.

When Jean came to find him he was reading a book out loud, one far beyond his grade level, but he was reading in his Mikey voice. She stopped to listen and realized it was "Tom Sawyer".

"Tom appeared on the sidewalk with a bucket of whitewash and a long-handled brush. He surveyed the fence and all the gladness left him..."

"You're reading Tom Sawyer?"

"No, Mikey is reading Tom Sawyer to me. He's getting very good."

"Do you read to Mikey?"

"We take turns. It is hard at school because he hates the baby books they give us to read."

"Come along to lunch. The Wells will be coming by soon."

"Can I take my bike?"

"Not this time. You can't ride it in the park. They've just posted the new law: no bikes or skate boards. "

Teddy sat at the kitchen table and ate his peanut butter and jelly sandwich.

"What does peanut butter and jelly taste like?" Mikey asked.

"Can't you tell? You seem to know everything else?" Teddy answered.

"I can't feel what you do. I used to, but not now."

"Well, it's sticky and gooey and sticks to the roof of my mouth."

"Teddy, stop talking to yourself," Jean broke in, "The Wells will be coming by shortly, so finish up."

Betty Wells, Jean's closest friend, lived a few houses away. Young, attractive and full of energy, she had been a social worker before her children were born and still worked part time. Jean often took care of Billy for her; in fact Billy and Teddy had been friends almost from birth.

Betty was a born optimist and firmly believed that Teddy would soon outgrow Mikey. She thought Teddy had a marvelous imagination but had cautioned Billy not to speak 'Mikey talk' in order to help Teddy grow up and make friends at school. Since Billy believed that Mikey was real and "cool" he did not heed her except to be sure she didn't hear him talking to Mikey. Betty was curious about what might be underlying circumstances that made Teddy rely on Mikey when other children had long forgotten their imaginary friends.

When Teddy heard them coming up the

walk, he grabbed his coat and ran outside. Bowser bounded along beside him.

"Hi, Billy, let's go." And the two little boys ran down the walk and headed toward the park two blocks away. Their mothers followed leisurely, discussing the latest problems of childrearing.

"Honestly, Betty, I don't know what I am going to do...." That was enough for Teddy.

"Race ya to the park, Billy. Bet I can swing higher then you can."

"No you can't. I can swing almost up to the bar..."

And they ran toward the park, Bowser barking happily along side. As they headed for the swings Teddy heard his mother's voice:

"Be careful. Don't swing high, you might get hurt." But they weren't listening.

"Come on, Teddy, you can beat Billy. Swing higher, swing higher. We can fly...I feel free..."

"Slow down, Teddy..." his mother called.

"Higher, Teddy, higher... " Mikey

commanded.

Then something happened and Teddy was flying through the air. The last thing he heard was his mother's voice and Bowser barking frantically.

"How many times have I asked him not to swing so high? If I'd only stopped him...He loves to take risks, and then blames it on Mikey. Oh, Betty, I hope he'll be okay; he's so little." Jean wept and wrung her hands, unable to sit still in the waiting room at the hospital.

"Jean, Dr. Bagley is with him and will see he gets the best care." Betty tried to sooth her.

"His poor little head...it's so misshapen anyhow. Maybe now they can find out why."

Since shortly after his birth Teddy's head appeared lopsided. At first it was thought to have been molded by the difficult birth and the use of forceps. As he grew older, a bump high on his forehead remained and seemed to enlarge. It gave him an odd look. Kids in his first grade class nicknamed him 'the alien.'

Jean paced back and forth in the empty hospital waiting room. She'd watched them wheel the gurney with Teddy down the hall of the ER and through the doors, but they stopped her from following.

"He's so little..." She pleaded to no avail.

Suddenly the waiting-room door swung open; Lloyd Thompson strode in, out of breath and looking very concerned. Usually impeccably dressed, his tie was askew, and his coat thrown carelessly over his arm.

"I got here are soon as possible. What happened? Where's Teddy? Have you spoken to the doctors?"

He put his arm around Jean but looked over her head at Betty for answers. Little Billy sucked his thumb and buried his head in his mother's skirt.

"I'm sure the doctors will be here soon. They were going to give Teddy an MRI and CAT scan to check him for injuries."

Betty liked Lloyd but always felt awkward with him as he'd made it clear that he had little faith in social workers. He considered them nosey do-gooders.

"What actually happened, Betty?" Lloyd

asked.

Billy spoke up: "Mikey made Teddy swing too high and...and the chain broke." He put his thumb back in his mouth and hid his head again.

Lloyd eased Jean down onto a couch and sat next to her. She was shaking, crying, and unable to talk except to repeat.

"I told him not to swing high; I told him to slow down..."

"The kids always love the park swings and generally are quite good. We watch them carefully, but today Teddy seemed more energized than usual. Jean cautioned Teddy several times, but he didn't pay attention. He just kept going higher and higher, and screaming with glee. Suddenly one of die chains snapped and he flew off hitting his head as he landed. It knocked him out. Someone called the police, and they brought an ambulance. He didn't wake up before we got here. Dr. Bagley was called, too, and met us at the door of the ER."

Lloyd comforted his wife but also chided her.

"Jean, you know how wild Teddy can get. You've got to be firmer with him."

"It was Mikey's fault," Billy said, looking up again. "Mikey made him do it."

Betty hushed her son.

"Now that you're here, Lloyd, I think we had better go home. Please let us know how Teddy is and if there is anything we can do to help. Come, Billy." She hugged Jean and headed toward the door.

"Mikey's bad," Billy said as they left.

Time moved slowly as the Thompsons waited in the Green Room. "Why do they always paint waiting-rooms green?" Jean wondered glancing up at the clock. It has been at least two hours. "What's taking so long?"

The door swung open and a large family group filed in, settling on the remaining seats and lining the walls. They chattered like starlings, all talking at the same time and not listening.

"I told you to stay away from those boys."

"That gang's good for nothing. Why did you take your brother?"

"Who had the gun? What was the fight about...."

The door opened again and the group was summoned. They rose en mass and exited.

Jean had stopped crying, and Lloyd had become calm. Dr. Bagley came in dressed in hospital greens, mask hanging down.

"Teddy's going to be okay, Jean and Lloyd. Please follow me to the office. Dr. Ames will be joining us and Dr. Chalfont. We're lucky he was in the hospital today. He is a wonderful neurosurgeon." They followed him through the door and along a labyrinth of hallways to his large bright office where they were introduced to a team of doctors.

Dr. Chalfont began: "With your permission, we would like to operate on Teddy today. It is not a simple concussion. He has a lot of pressure on his brain. We've run several tests and a very interesting condition has been revealed that may explain the shaping of Teddy's head, his headaches, and possibly his "invisible' friend."

"Will he be alright?" Jean asked, "Will he be normal?"

"We'll have to see how the operation goes,

but I think he will do very well. He's healthy and strong."

"What did the tests show?" Lloyd asked.

"There is a mass, a growth at the front of Teddy's brain. It is pressing on his frontal lobe and probably may be the cause of his headaches and unusual behavior."

Dr. Bagley turned to Dr. Ames, who said: "Going over your son's file we discovered that your pregnancy started out as twins. Along about the third month there was only one fetus; the second one had disappeared or been absorbed. I think the lump on Teddy's cerebral cortex may be the remains of the twin; in other words, his vanished twin. We hope to find out when we go in and will remove whatever it is. We will reshape the front of his head so that it looks normal."

"Teddy's is being prepared for the operation, now. It may take several hours. Go home if you like, and I will call you as soon as we know." Dr. Ames said.

"No, I prefer to wait here." Jean said; Lloyd nodded in agreement.

While Teddy was being prepared for surgery, he became aware of distant voices fading in and out. Within, he conversed with Mikey.

"Now you've done it Mikey. Where are we?"

"Your fault, Teddy, Mom told you not to swing so high."

"You told me to go higher."

"What happened? We were flying, and everything went black."

A voice broke through from outside: "Will you look at that...it looks like a tiny body with no head. It's curled up tight...careful, now..."

"What's happening, Teddy?...I, ooooh." Mikey's voice faded. Teddy felt suddenly alone.

"Mikey? Mikey? Where are you?"

That was the last thing Teddy remembered. He awoke in a strange room and looked up at a circle of concerned faces...his parents and strangers in masks.

"How do you feel, Teddy?" Dr. Bagley

asked.

"My head hurts."

"How many fingers am I holding up?"

"Three. Why? Mom, where am I?"

"Do you remember what happened?"

"No...you promised we could go to the park..." Teddy drifted off into a deep sleep.

Back in the office, the doctors gathered with the Thompsons.

"The surgery went very smoothly;" Dr. Chalfont said, "And we were able to reshape his head. Providing there is no infection and if the healing goes smoothly, his head will appear normal with no bump on his forehead."

"What happens now? Will Mikey go away?" Jean asked.

"Teddy's headaches should stop now. The cause of the pressure, his parasitic twin, has been removed. He will probably be as normal as any other boy his age. He will have to rest for the next few months until he has healed. No sports, particularly contact sports. We will have a protective helmet made for him. But next fall he may go back to school. He may never remember what happened."

"So his invisible friend has been removed. "Lloyd said, "Should we bury it?"

"With your permission we would like to keep it. It would be a great help toward studying how this happened. It is unusual but not unique. Commonly, a twin is absorbed in the early weeks of pregnancy; some become parasitic such as in Teddy's case, and some simply disappear."

Dr. Bagley added, "Perhaps it is best not to talk about what happened with Teddy, unless he questions you. When he is older he will be more able to understand it."

Teddy went home and spent the summer healing. He played with Billy who told him of the accident and eventually asked him how Mikey was.

"Mikey went away," was all that Teddy would say.

In the fall Teddy entered a new school and did well. Indeed his headaches had all but gone and he enjoyed simply being a normal little boy.

It wasn't until he was about thirteen that he began having occasional dreams about another boy that looked just like him. Then one day he heard a small familiar voice within:

"I'm ba-ack," it taunted. *"I'm hiding."*

"Mikey? Where are you?"
"You'll find out"

-- *Rosamond C. Hughes*

The members of the Writers' Circle look forward to the future chapters of "Invisible Friend" that are germinating in the imagination of Roz Hughes.

Looking for Bob Marley

THE GHOST SHIP

It was June 1976. As we approached the pier in New Jersey, we saw a large rusty hulk that resembled something out of an old vintage film, with a ghost ship appearing out of a misty fog and the only sounds in the night were of waves lapping at the hull and a lonely foghorn.

The name "Gydinia" and the Polish flag, were painted on the topside of the main smokestack. This rusty hulk was mine and I had to claim her. My youngest daughter, Tien said, "Ma, you cannot go anywhere on that!" I tried to re-assure her; "I'm sure it's not as bad as it looks." Inside my trembling core I knew that booking passage on that freighter was a real bad mistake.

As soon as I stepped inside of the ship, all of my trepidation disappeared. The interior was immaculate. The walls, counters, and fixtures were covered with beautiful dark polished wood panels. It was like being in an old library without books. All was well.

The Gydinia was a passenger freighter, which accommodated up to twelve passengers. It was fully booked. There were ten adults aboard, a pre teen-aged Asian girl, named Lin, and a ten-year old boy, named William. The boy became my buddy while we explored every inch of that ship and I taught him how to play a few simple chords on my guitar. Lin played the flute. Sometimes Lin and I would do a duet of our own composition, while William would beat out a rhythm on the table when we had our jam sessions. They were great kids; we had a ball.

My friends, Dee and Beverly Moats were waiting for me on the dock in Tillsbury, England. At that time a slow boat to England to spend the summer with dear friends in Buckhamshire (a London suburb) was just what I needed to de-stress and regain the balance in my life.

I would play "If I Were a Carpenter" and Dee would sing at the top of his lungs then clap for himself. Bev and Dee adopted a beautiful little Indian girl, named Paulina. She was four years old and wore eyeglasses, which just made her more adorable. When she met me she said, in her perfect English accent, "Oh look Mummy, Marcia's brown, like me." Those months I spent with the Moats in

Buckinghamshire were some of the best moments of my life.

During my stay in "Bucks," I was looking through an entertainment supplement of the local newspaper because I heard that Bob Marley was appearing somewhere in London, and I very much wanted to catch his performance.

While Looking for Bob Marley, I came across a tiny advertisement promoting a twenty-eight day barebones tour through Morocco. It read, "See the real Morocco, travel with other like-minded explorers, by van, hovercraft and ferry. We'll be roughing it, so leave your fancy clothes at home." $200!

I WAS GOING! Once more I leapt without looking.

THE VAN FROM HELL

The morning of our departure I was a little tired from partying the night before with some friends from Ghana who were visiting family in London. I arrived at the meeting place a little late. There were nine passengers, two tour guides, Mike and Jillian, and Mike's seven-year old daughter Jenny, waiting for me, in the van.

There was something different about the van; it didn't look like the dandy van in the photograph Mike and Jillian showed me when I met with them to finalize arrangements for the trip. They claimed that the van was being serviced. The vehicle standing before me was an old patched wreck. When I looked into the van from the only door at the rear of the vehicle, I saw a van full of angry white people.

My first inclination was to get the hell out of there. I thought they were angry with me for being late, then, I got a good look at the seating arrangement inside the van. I couldn't believe my eyes. Instead of individual seats with nice high backs, like in the photo, there were two long wooden crate-like constructions that had storage space underneath the plywood board on top. Upholstered cushions were attached to the plywood to sit on. There was a padded bolster backrest as long as the seating units were, that was somehow secured to the inside wall of the van on either side. I wanted to wake up from that bad dream.

My fellow travelers were sitting facing each other with their knees either touching or wedged to one side to accommodate a couple of guys who were over six feet tall, with long knees. It was just too unreal!

The thought of riding that way for twenty-eight days, was incomprehensible. I looked around and said, "Oh what the hell, since it can't get any worse, it has got to get better, right?" Then there was a perfect British female voice heard from inside the van, "We had all better pray."

Since we were sitting facing each other, the tall guy's like James and Nicholas had to stagger the seating arrangement because two tall people couldn't fit across from each other. The sight of us trying to arrange our bodies like sardines in a can, made us all laugh. We were determined to make it work, or so we thought.

I was so dumbfounded at our traveling accommodations that I didn't even say good morning or introduce myself, even though I was sure they knew who I was, being the only American and "a person of color," on that trip. As I reluctantly stepped into the back of the "Van from Hell," I said, "Ah Jesus, what the hell kind of trip is this going to be?"

We introduced ourselves, then, Nicholas shouted to our drivers, "OK, let's get on with it, besides, if we sit any closer we'll have to get married to give the baby a name." At that point we couldn't have imagined what additional calamities the gods had in store for us, but they sure did.

CHECKPOINT

Traveling through Morocco, we had to go through a checkpoint when entering each new region. At the first checkpoint, the soldiers on guard looked very serious and a little threatening. Our usually loud, jovial group became very quiet as the soldier with a rifle over his shoulder approached the van and asked the driver for our passports. Mike, our driver/tour guide, handed them over to the soldier. He called off the names of the passengers, and, when he saw my passport he said to Mike, "Jameson, where is Jameson; Tell her to come down." You could hear a pin drop in the van from hell. I quickly replied, "OK, I'm coming." I whispered to my new best friend, Samantha, "If I don't come back, tell my girls that I love them, and that I died for my country." Samantha didn't think it was at all funny.

I followed the soldier into a building, then into the office of Colonel Aziz.

He was not very tall or what you would call handsome, but with his dark swarthy looks and impeccable uniform, he could be considered at least "dashing."

I couldn't believe how cool it was in there; I sighed with pleasure. My "mates" and I were badly parched from the relentless heat, which was usually over one hundred and ten degrees during the day. There were times when our lips would stick to our teeth when we smiled, and the dry air in our throats would make us choke. Sometimes we rode in that van from hell (with no air-conditioning) for hours, with wet towels over our head and shoulders to prevent dehydration.

Whenever we approached a stream or oasis; just like an old western movie, we would all jump out of the van fully clothed, and throw ourselves into any body of water nearby. Then we would get back in the van, soaking wet, and continue on our way.

Colonel Aziz introduced himself to me and said, with obvious curiosity, "So you are Afro-Sister, yes?"

I said "yes", trying not to show my amusement.

He came closer, with a really serious look on his face, and said, "Tell me, do you know Aretha Franklin?" I tried not to react in-appropriately by screaming or laughing; I hoped my mouth wasn't hanging open.

"No, not personally" I said.

"She is great soul sister singer, yes?' "Absolutely, she's the best."

"But assuredly, you know the great Muslim man, Mohammed Ali?"

"Yes I have met him, we Americans are very proud of him."

"There are slaves in America?'

"No, not anymore, but there is still trouble between the races."

"People are poor?"

"Some, yes."

"But plenty rich?"

"Yes, some."

After pausing, he whispered to me, "Watch out for them", motioning with his head in the direction of the window where we could see the van. I knew he meant my fellow travelers. My "interrogation" was turning into a real eye-opener.

Realizing that I was standing the whole time, Colonel Aziz apologized and invited me to sit down. Then I started wondering, "What the hell is he going to do to me now?"

He said, "Would you like a cold Coca Cola?" Little did he know that I would have given him my first and second-born for anything resembling a cold drink.

"Yes, thank you so very much," I groveled. He sent a young office boy to get my drink. He was back in minutes. I drank it all down without stopping, and had to stifle a gigantic burp burning in my stomach while Col. Aziz tried not to laugh.

The colonel then leaned in close to me, and I thought, "Oh shit, here it comes, the invitation to join his harem." Then he whispered, "Would you like to change monies?" I tried not to shout, "Hell Yeah!" He went into the other office and came back with a handful of francs. He gave me a really a good rate.

I said, "You're very kind. Thank you so much." I was still "stroking" him, just in case I did end up in his Harem.

He asked me where we were headed. I told him, "Rabat, Fez, Casablanca, Marakesh, Quarzazate, Chaouen, Agadir, Zagora, Ksar es Souk, and other places I can't remember. He looked surprised. Then he wrote out a list of names and telephone numbers of government officials in comparable positions to his, and numerous relatives and friends of his all over Morocco. He said, "If you have any trouble, go to my people and tell them I said to help you." I was truly overwhelmed at his kindness. I said, "Vous etes tres charmand, mon Ami. I could tell that he was impressed by my attempt to flatter him with my fractured French. He said, "vous etes tres jolie, Madame." I was thoroughly charmed and would have gladly joined his harem.

We shook hands and he must have given me a blessing because I heard him say "Allah;" little did I know then how much I would need that little blessing.

I had been "interrogated" for at least forty-five minutes, and my "mates" were growing worried. When I got back into the van, they hovered, while trying not to show their concern. They asked;

"Marcia, did they harm you?" "Was it awful for you?"

"Why the bloody hell did it take so long?" Nicholas asked.

"Are you alright dear?"

"Did they put their hands on you?"

"It's all over now, so no worries."

"What did they do to you?"

The devil was in me as I replied, somberly, "I'd rather not talk about it."

As I climbed into the van, stepping over an assortment of legs, I got hugs and pats; then I really felt wicked. I don't know how Samantha knew I lied, but she did. She whispered to me in her perfect upper class Queen's English, "You are so naughty! What really went on in there?"

I said, "Girl, I had an ice-cold Coca Cola, got my money changed at a great rate, and was given a list of names of important people all over Morocco, to contact if I need help. I made out like a bandit!" We covered our mouths to muffle the laughs.

Samantha asked, "Did he get into your knickers for all of that?" I replied, "Hey, for that cold Coca Cola, he could have gotten into mine, and I would have offered him yours too." And so it began, our Moroccan adventure.

ENOUGH IS ENOUGH

Just halfway through our trip my fascination with those exotic and mysterious places had worn off, and I was wearing out. I was tired of the heat, the dust, sleeping on the ground with crawling insects making a meal of me, crapping in a hole in the ground with a tall piece of galvanize wrapped around it. We couldn't bring ourselves to call it a Toilet, or a Loo. You needed high-heeled rubber boots to even step into that shithouse. When we had to venture into one of those "places," we would put Vicks Vaporub in our nostrils so as not to spend any extra time in there, throwing up.

Like several of my fellow travelers, I had the "Trots", off and on, and sometimes Samantha's legs wouldn't work. They had to be massaged to get the feeling back. Just five months before the trip, she had back surgery as a result of a bout with bone cancer, she had confided in me.

Things were deteriorating quickly between our motley crew, and tempers flared more often. We all had some ailment or another that needed attention: blisters, bites, sores, scratches, diarrhea, upset stomachs and such. Every part of our bodies ached from sleeping on the ground, or on rooftops, and sitting cramped up in the van for hours, while Mike tried to make his (alleged) drug connections.

We all felt very privileged to have a certified nurse on-board. Samantha was a godsend. She did triage on a regular basis. She was able to buy almost any kind of medication in Morocco and in Spain. Samantha improvised, using some of our ladies sanitary napkins, to compress boils and cover badly oozing blisters.

One of our guys went hiking for several hours with no socks on underneath his brand new leather Timberland boots; I think it was the brilliant fellow with the Diplomatic Corps, that ended up with his feet wrapped in sanitary napkins. Some of our crew needed shots for infections, and all kind of ointments were applied to all parts of our worn-out bodies. "MASH" had nothing on us.

The discomfort and grime were really getting to us, and, I was running out of steam. Samantha's back was hurting and she was limping quite a bit, but she refused to stay behind at the campsite, when we went to visit the tannery in Fez.

On the way to the tannery, Madelene and Marianne walked ahead of Samantha and I looking for good bargains at the shops and stalls in the Souk. It was a busy thoroughfare with all kinds of beautiful wares for sale, like, woven baskets, native silver and copper jewelry, rugs and kaftans of all colors. One shop had the most wonderful assortment of musical instruments, which looked like works of art. I wanted one of each.

We heard someone shouting and there was some commotion ahead of us. It was Marianne and Madelene. Marianne told us that two local teenage boys came towards them, then quick like lightning each boy grabbed at one of the girls' crotch, then ran like hell, laughing with glee, disappearing into the crowd. Madelene just stood there in shock and Marianne screamed, "You bloody perverts." That's when we all began to laugh.

Marianne was in her twenties. She was tall and tanned with long sun-bleached hair and blue eyes; a natural beauty. She was pretty and tough. An Australian, she worked as a writer with a nature-watch magazine, but you could tell that she could hold her own with the guys. I would pick her brains about everything Australian, just to hear her speak.

Madelene was the dearest person. Every morning, she cooked porridge on her small camping stove for all those who wanted some, and sprinkled raisins on top. She was a teacher in one of the toughest middle schools in London. It was hard to conceive how that gentle soul could handle a classroom full of less than congenial teenagers.

Madelene had the look of a runner, long and lean. She was pale in spite of her efforts to tan. Her dark shoulder length hair was worn straight with bangs, which highlighted her pale blue eyes. Even though she was at least thirty years old, she had a look of innocence about her; probably because of her kind and gentle demeanor. She was deeply concerned about any injustice in the world, especially against children.

The dye pits were on the roof of the tannery. You could smell it way before you could see it. The awful smell made me feel sick. Samantha and I decided not to enter the tannery. As we leaned against the stone wall outside, trying to catch our breath, without breathing, we heard a man's voice shouting, "Attencion, Attencion!" It got louder and louder, then we saw a man on foot leading a donkey with two large baskets of fermenting cabbage tied to the donkey's back, hanging from each side. Fermented cabbage was used at the Tannery to "cure" the leather.

The donkey slipped and slid in the wet manure coating the gray stones underfoot; as it came to pass us on that narrow street, we flattened ourselves as hard as we could against the wall.

The unsteady beast tried to regain its balance, as the handler struck the donkey again and again with a stick. The cabbage was being flung back and forth with some spilling on the ground as the putrid droplets sprayed everything in its path, including us. We covered our faces until the donkey passed, wiping our faces and trying not to "retch."

At that point I didn't know whether to cry or throw up. Samantha said, "Let's smoke a fag, that should help with the smell." We passed that short brown Moroccan cigarette back and forth, like a treasured stick of marijuana. We didn't even inhale; we just blew smoke in each other's face. After coughing and choking for about ten minutes, we decided to get the hell out of there.

Samantha was limping and I was getting

some slight chest pains; we were both on the verge of tears. I said, "Samantha, I can't do this anymore".

"Nor can I," she said, "but we must."

I said, "What the hell am I doing over here? I should be somewhere all dressed up, sitting on a barstool in a jazz joint in Harlem, wearing my Audrey Hepburn sunglasses, holding a long cigarette holder, drinking a frosted glass of champagne," I whined.

Even though we were both on the verge of tears, we had to laugh at ourselves. Samantha said, "You are really round the bend, old girl." She made, "being crazy" sound like a compliment.

It seemed like we had been walking through the marketplace for over an hour. Each vendor's stall or shop looked just like every other one we passed. WE WERE LOST! Eventually we came to the end of the marketplace and we could see the exit. We limped towards the exit only to see a police barricade. There was a policeman there, not letting anyone in or out for some reason.

The policeman said, in English, "You cannot pass!" The thought of having to go back in the direction we had just come from made me weak in the knees. I was prepared to go to jail just to have a drink of water and get off my feet. Samantha definitely couldn't last much longer. I was getting ready to tell the policeman that, if we were not allowed to leave, we would need an ambulance.

Standing outside the marketplace behind the barricade was a small crowd of people, mostly women, seeking entry. Samantha looked like she was going to pass out and went to sit on the barricade while I went to speak to the policeman. I spoke as quietly as I could manage, (considering that I was "a woman on the edge"). "Please let us through," I begged, "We've been lost for over an hour and my friend is sick, as you can see."

Before the policeman even had a chance to reply, the group of women behind the barricade started yelling at the policeman shaking their hands in protest, some shouting, "Let them go, let them go," (in French and English) pointing to Samantha, who was sitting on the barricade with her head in her hands. He was being well chastised. "OK, go, go, go", he said. We thanked the ladies on our way to a taxi.

As we stretched out in the taxi, Samantha said, "Dear God, will it ever end?"

"Will what ever end?" I asked.

She said; "The madness, the heat, the constant praying on those bloody loudspeakers day and night, and all the craziness in that damn van. You would think, if they really are smuggling hashish in the van, using us for cover, the least they could do is to offer us a little bit of it, so we can, fucking cope."

"Now there's a thought," I said.

AN UNEXPECTED VISITOR

We were halfway through our "Moroccan adventure." At the last campsite before heading for the desert, we were all bustling around getting ready to get on the road before the sun came up. Samantha was still asleep; which was unusual for her.

Samantha usually slept on her side in a fetal position to relieve her back pain. We tried to wake her up, but she didn't respond. Amanda started shaking her, with great force, calling her name. I shouted, "don't shake her like that, she has a fused spine, it's really bad." They looked at me in disbelief. Until then, I was the only one who knew about her health problems.

Nicholas and the other "Mates" gathered around. I cautioned them to support her body while slowly, gently turning her over. When they had turned her over and we saw her swollen face, Madelene screamed, "Dear God, she's been stung by a scorpion!" Having traveled in similar environments, she knew what she was talking about.

Her face was red and swollen and her eyes were swollen shut. She was listless and seemed to be floating in and out of consciousness. Nicholas picked Samantha up and ran to the campsite office. One of the employees immediately took them to the hospital/clinic nearby.

Fanny asked, "Where's the bloody van?" As usual, the van and our driver, Mike, were missing; which further convinced us that he and Jillian were trafficking drugs.

I collected Samantha's pocketbook and personal items from her sleeping bag, and shouted to anyone standing nearby, "I need to go to the hospital; can anyone give me a ride?" A young man standing nearby offered me a ride on his motorcycle. My concern for my friend was greater than my fear of being kidnapped, or robbed. Although any fool could see that it would be a waste of time to rob any of us.

He looked to be in his twenty's and quite handsome. I assumed that he was Moroccan. He extended his hand and said, "Come, I will take you," he spoke perfect English, and had a nice smile. He was dressed in a t-shirt with a sports logo on it, well-fitting blue jeans and sandals. The watch on his wrist appeared to be a "Rolex," and his motorcycle looked new. He gave the appearance of someone with a comfortable lifestyle. I thought, "Why the hell not, so far nothing about this trip had been ordinary, or predictable."

I slung Samantha's bag over one of my shoulders, and my bag over the other one, then climbed onto the back of the motorcycle behind the young stranger. Before I could even get settled, he took my hands and wrapped my arms tightly around his waist, he said "Hold on," as he patted my butt, pretending to make sure I was securely seated.

I chose to ignore it the first two times he did that, but with the third pat, I slapped him lightly on his head and said, "Stop that, I'm old enough to be your mother." "That's OK," he said, laughing. I gave him another little slap on the head and said, "Behave."

We got there really fast. I had to close my eyes while we raced through those dusty, pitted, roads, to the clinic. I was really grateful for the ride and thanked him over and over. When I offered him some money, he refused to accept it. He said, "I hope your friend will be well soon and that you will have a safe trip here in my country. I gave him a little hug, and said, " Au revoir, and, Merci beaucoup. He waved and sped off on his motorcycle.

I was taken to what I assumed was the emergency room of the clinic/hospital. The clinic was very old, and bleak. Samantha was on some sort of a gurney, with Nicholas standing by holding her hand. She was still listless and her face was quite swollen. She was in a panic, talking very fast, "Nicholas, tell him not to raise my legs for any reason because my spine is fused, quickly, quickly!" Nicholas relayed the information to the doctor in the most perfect French, which made him all the more dashing.

Without making any eye contact or even explaining what he was about to do, the doctor headed towards the instrument sterilizer. Samantha pulled me towards her and whispered, "Make sure the water in the sterilizer is boiling, hurry!"

I walked towards the doctor's back as quietly

as I could and peeked over his shoulder. The water was bubbling away. As he took a needle from the sterilizer he gave me a chilling look, "Yes, do you want something?" he asked. I smiled and said, "Just curious." As I backed away from his frightening glare, a chill went through me; I felt real fear.

The doctor gave Samantha an injection of an anti-allergy serum. Her face started to change color and the swelling began to subside immediately. I was amazed at how quickly the medication worked. Nicholas asked the doctor, "Will she be alright?" He answered, reluctantly, without any emotion at all, and took his time to answer, "I think so," We three got the hell out of there as fast as we could.

I couldn't bring myself to think what would have happened if we were somewhere in the desert.

Samantha was still quite weak. We tried to make her as comfortable as we could in the van, as we headed for the desert.

Everyone had rightly assumed that neither Samantha nor I, were going to the desert. We were going to quit while we were 'almost' ahead.

IN THE KITCHEN

Samantha and I were dropped off at a small hotel near the desert with the understanding that the others would pick us up on their way back. We hugged our "mates," who by that time were "extended family," and gave them whatever supplies we didn't need as we bid them goodbye. Even though the hotel was old, it was cleaner than most we had stayed in. Just to rest in a clean bed was a luxury. We were exhausted.

We rested for about an hour. Then when I checked our rucksacks for energy bars and water, I remembered that ants had gotten into our food supply at the last campsite, and the provisions that we all shared, like, canned cheese, fruit, tuna fish, pickled vegetables, and soda crackers, were in the van on the way to the desert. With all of the day's excitement we hadn't eaten. We were starving!

I remembered seeing a small cafe down the road a little way from the hotel as we were approaching the hotel earlier. I decided to venture down the road in search of food.

When I arrived at the cafe I saw a middle-aged man in a blue jalabia and a matching kofi on his head. I assumed that he was the owner. He was in the process of closing two large wooden doors that were attached to a terracotta archway. I shouted, "Oh no, please, please don't close!" My desperation was obvious, "Sorry I'm closed," he said In French.

I begged him in my most pathetic French, to please, "please, give me some food for my friend who was bitten by a scorpion." That got his attention. "Scorpion" he said. "Scorpion est tres mal, votre ami est mort?" "No, but, mon ami est tres, tres, faim, and jai tres, tres, faim aussi, sil vous plait, Can we have some food to eat, sil vous plait?" I pleaded. I pantomimed with my hand to my mouth like I was eating, then, put my hands in "a prayer" position. I could see that he was trying hard not to laugh.

He opened the gigantic wooden doors. Then he sighed and mumbled something in French, indicating his reluctance at having to do the right thing.

I was feeling pretty pleased with myself until he said, (in French), you have to come to the kitchen and help me cook. I looked at him and said, "Pardon, jai suis non comprendre." Without missing a beat he replied with glee, "Ah oui, vous comprenez, vous comprenez".

I tried very hard to look confused but he wasn't buying it. He walked towards the open door to the cafe, then turned around and beaconed me with a flick of his head, "Allez, allez", and just like an obedient wife, I followed.

We passed through the indoor dining space,

which was quite charming. The walls were terracotta with decorative tiles in some areas and the archway leading to the kitchen had intricate designs carved along the edge. You could tell that the cafe was old, but quite lovely.

As we walked towards the kitchen, I looked around to see where another exit was; there was none. Then I scanned the kitchen quickly to see where the knives were kept, "Just in case." I sized him up and decided I could "take him down," if I needed to. He was watching me watching him and laughed, I laughed too. Who was I fooling?

He led me to a long wooden table with stools and invited me to sit down. My new kitchen boss took a bowl of boiled and peeled potatoes from the refrigerator and placed them on the table before me. He took one of the potatoes and showed me how to dice them. I took the knife indignantly and said, (with an attitude), "I know how to dice potatoes," he replied something in French that sounded like, "OK, then dice them, Professeur," as he pinched my cheek.

He heated up a large circular frying pan, then poured a good amount of olive oil in, and threw a handful of assorted herbs into the hot oil. The smell was absolutely tantalizing. He gave me peppers and onions to chop while he diced some other vegetables that were foreign to me.

I asked many questions about the vegetables he was dicing, then while picking up vegetables, roots, and some sort of chives to smell, I asked, "What are these called?" He told me the names of every one of them and described how they grew. He said it all in French but he was easy to understand even though I didn't recognize all of the words. He seemed pleased at my efforts, then, he pinched my cheek again. I thought to myself, "OK, that's two!"

I was instructed to crack open about seven eggs in the bowl he had placed before me; then he demonstrated how to beat them. Gently pushing his hand away, I said, with an attitude, "I know how beat some damn eggs!" He laughed and pinched my cheek again. Unintentionally, I must have been turning him on, and that was the last thing I wanted to do, anywhere, in Morocco.

As the magnificent omelet cooked, I had a chance to look around the kitchen. It was beautiful; all terracotta and tile. There was an assortment of elaborately decorated plates, bowls, cups, saucers, copper pots, and teapots with decorated tile handles, on the shelves. There were lanterns made from hammered copper and stacks of rust colored ceramic plates of all sizes. Every piece was a work of art.

I told "Monsieur" that I was an artist and how delighted I was to be in his beautiful kitchen. He started to explain how the ceramics were made, and when I told him that I had made some bowls and other ceramic items on a pottery wheel (as I demonstrated), he seemed very impressed. That whole scene was surreal, but also very natural. It occurred to me that maybe in some ways we are more alike than different.

The combination of herbs and spices sizzling in the pan created the most wonderful aroma. My cheerful Kitchen Boss watched me as I inhaled every essence of magic in that pan. I decided that he could pinch my cheek anytime he wanted to.

He used a large flat wooden spatula to retrieve that fabulous omelet and placed it in a large circular ceramic plate. Then he put two large spheres of warm pita bread on top of the omelet and placed a tent shaped ceramic lid on top. "Voila", he said, as he handed me the plate. I was overwhelmed with gratitude. "Combien?" I asked, He told me the cost of that incredible meal, which was less than two American dollars. It was obvious that he gave us a special price. I tried to give him a little extra money but he pushed it away, saying, "Non, c'est specialement pour votre ami et vous. I told him that I would bring the plate back tomorrow, and, thanked him once again. He said, "Bon appétit."

When Samantha saw that gigantic omelet she shrieked with lust. I placed that plate, (as big as a flying saucer), in the middle of the bed and we pounced on it like two starving wolves. To this day that was the best meal I have ever eaten.

We must have fallen asleep. The empty plate was still there in the middle of the bed; crumbs and specks of food were everywhere.

It was around ten thirty at night, when we heard a knock at the door. "Who is it?" I asked," Monsieur du la cafe," he replied. "Un moment." I said, quickly putting a shirt on over my wrap, then picked up the empty ceramic plate and opened the door. And there he was!

"Monsieur" was dressed in gray suit pants, a white shirt, dark tie and, a light summer jacket. His thick black hair was oiled and parted on the side combed across his forehead. It looked like his moustache had been oiled and combed too. Even though he was not a tall or slender man, he looked quite handsome in his "Colonial clothing." I told him how nice he looked, and, he blushed. I introduced him to Samantha. He said that he was glad to see her feeling better. Samantha thanked him for the wonderful food; in French, with a British accent.

I handed him his plate and as he gently pushed it away, he said something that sounded like he was asking me out on a date! I said, "pardon", pretending once again that I didn't understand him. He gave me a sly look and said, "Vous comprenez," pointing a finger at me, smiling. Then he put one of his hands in the middle of his chest and extended the other one, rocking from side to side, imitating a couple dancing, and said, "We dance, yes?" I thanked him for the invitation and explained to him that my stomach was still, "Tres mal", and I was, "Tres, tres, fatigue," and also, my friend was still not feeling well.

He took the plate, looking quite dejected. I really felt bad for having to turn him down, but my stomach really wasn't "predictable" yet, and since I had just eaten one half of a flying saucer; who knows what would have happened, later, and also, I wasn't totally comfortable going on a date with a virtual stranger, in Morocco, no less. I told him that we would come to the cafe the next day to have lunch with him. Once again, we thanked him for everything. Samantha teased, "Marcia, he was quite a darling little man, and not bad looking either."

The patio at the cafe was occupied with an assortment of Moroccan men smoking their hooka pipes and cigarettes while sipping hot sweet tea. As we approached the cafe, you could hear a pin drop. Samantha grabbed my hand and whispered, "What's wrong with them?" Are we going to be OK?" I whispered, "We should have worn our veils,"

"Monsieur" soon came to our rescue. He had on his traditional clothes, which seemed a little more ornate than the outfit he had on the previous day. Our host was dressed up and obviously showing off a little. He kissed our hands and offered us a seat at his table, which was in the center of the patio, for all to see. He had cooked tagine, (a meat and vegetable stew with spicy, pungent herbs), just for us. He remembered that I told him how much I loved tagine.

After he brought us our meal, "Monsieur" sat down with his chair to the side with his legs crossed, as he sipped tea. He did not eat with us, (we wondered about that later). We could tell right away that his demeanor had changed. He was a little cocky, but not at all offensive.

The male audience at that cafe was really creepy. They just stared at us like we were aliens from another planet, but it didn't keep us from devouring our delicious meal. "Monsieur" glanced around the cafe from time to time to see if he was being properly regarded, with his special guests.

His territorial demeanor didn't bother us at all. His, was the only friendly face we saw in that sea of testosterone. "Monsieur" wasn't Aladdin with a magic lamp, or a Caliph from the "Arabian Nights," but he was our hero. He earned it.

Within a few days, the gang in the van was back and we were off again on our crazy journey.

RENDEZVOUS

Halfway through our tour of Morocco, we had passed through Ksar es Souk, heading south towards the desert, coming across one of many arid, dusty, abandoned villages with crumbling adobe compounds. They looked like they had sprouted and grown from the rusty earth that surrounded them. The silence and desolation were somehow hypnotic; I remember how we whispered when we passed those ghosts.

The times when we could escape the chaos of our misguided tour, we would linger at the top of a hill accepting the gift of silence, while waiting for the sunset to give up it's blazing glow and invite the indigo of night. We devoured the peace and tranquility to help us through our next challenge, which was sure to come, all too soon.

Sometimes we had not only lost track of where we had been, but, also had no idea of where we were. What was even more pathetic is that it didn't matter to us anymore. We just wanted to go "home," to England.

Our initial excitement and anticipation of making wonderful discoveries in the "Real Morocco" had been snatched from us by the endless conflict with our tour guides/drug smugglers. God only knows what sinister rendezvous Mike had to keep, as we raced through one wonderful marketplace after another, begging him to stop so we could shop; to no avail. Our wonderful

"Moroccan Adventure" was quickly becoming more like a sequel to "The Lord of the Flies."

There we were, tethered to each other by fear of the unknown, in a broken down van driven by a madman.

SLEEPING WITH THE DEAD

The fatigue and frustration from just trying to cope from day to day in heat over one hundred degrees, was emotionally and physically debilitating. Our confrontational circumstances with our hosts, along with trying to stay out of some ancient Moroccan prison for aiding and abetting drug smugglers, had taken its toll on all of us.

We could usually find some morsel of humor under the most, dire circumstances, but our humor and congeniality had been replaced by resentment and total disdain for our tour guides, or whatever they were.

At first I couldn't quite understand why, "the guys," our fellow prisoners, didn't just grab Mike at one of our few rest stops, kick his ass, tie him up, chuck him into the back of the van and just take over the damn vehicle.

Mike and Jillian were always arguing. Jillian wanted to get out of their dysfunctional relationship, so we thought that, maybe she wouldn't stop us from hijacking the van, but we couldn't be sure. At times she was a total mystery to us. Jillian seemed like a really nice person with a lot of class. They were total opposites, or so we thought.

We had discussed the possible "hijacking" several times, and after venting and planning our "takeover" someone would say, "What about

Jenny?" Mike's seven-year old daughter, Jenny, was crazy about her father and we did not want to be the cause of hurting that sweet little girl for any reason, just her presence kept us civilized. We had to reconsider alternatives in dealing with Mike and Jillian.

After driving for hours into the night, at times we were forced to bed-down almost anywhere. Sometimes we had no choice but to stumble out of the van, and, "chuck rocks" to clear a smooth space for our sleeping bags.

There were times when I didn't know where I was when I woke up, with a backache and having to pee desperately. Then, reality would kick in, as I stumbled out of my sleeping bag looking for a bush or a boulder to hide behind to relieve myself, while trying not to Pee on my toes.

One windy morning we were awakened by the sound of goats baaing and the tinkle of tiny bells. If it were not for the goats, it could have been "Shangri-la."

We were being struck and poked with a stick by a little Moroccan man, who appeared to be a goat herder. He was hysterically screaming curses at us, in French. Nicholas tried in vain to calm the little guy, explaining that we meant him no harm.

The goats proceeded to walk all over us in our sleeping bags as well as our provisions nearby, while depositing their little "nuggets" everywhere.

By then we were wide-awake and getting a little pissed off. As he raised his stick again, Nicholas gently blocked his arm and said, "I don't think you want to do that again, Mate. The goat herder calmed down, and explained the problem.

Nicholas translated the little man's concerns to us. It seems like we had bedded-down in a graveyard. Nicholas said, "Probably with some of his relatives," which made us hysterical. We grabbed our gear and made a dash for the van. Fanny, our "wild card" on the trip said, in her strongest cockney accent, "Well that's the first time I've slept with the dead."

THE LONG TRIP HOME

Our driver/tour guide Mike, looked like a little leprechaun with stringy shoulder length hair and a big nose. He had such a strong cockney accent that sometimes even the "Brits" found it hard to understand him, especially when he was angry, which was too often. His girlfriend Jillian, was just the opposite of him. She was quite ladylike and gentle. Jillian was slightly taller than Mike (which wasn't hard). She had freckles, a sweet smile, and a head full of long curly brown hair. I thought she was quite lovely. She reminded me of an Elizabethan painting. Our band of gypsies spent a lot of time trying to figure them out; we never did.

The only thing that kept us from disintegrating into wild beasts was the presence of Mike's seven-year old daughter, Jenny. We all adored her. Mike and Jill weren't too big on cleanliness, for themselves or Jenny. Whenever we saw Jenny looking dirty and smelling a little funky, we ladies just took her over.

We washed her up every day and made sure she brushed her teeth. Sometimes after her bath, I would make her a wrap from a piece of my African fabric then splash her skin with a little Jene Nate cologne. She would smell her arms and say, "Oh Marcia, it's so lovely." We bought ribbons to put in her hair, and adorned her with some of our newly acquired Bedouin jewelry. She would scream with delight and dance around jangling her jewelry. Jenny was an absolute delight and brought out the best in all of us.

Even though Mike was "one crazy little fucker," surprisingly, he was the most gentle, patient, and loving father I've ever seen. He never yelled at his daughter or showed any displeasure at anything she did. He adored his little girl, and she knew it. We all speculated about who and where her mother was. Jillian was also very good to Jenny, it was obvious that she was loved.

Mike was becoming, more and more unstable by the minute. He was driving like the devil was chasing us, and wouldn't even stop to let us relieve ourselves. After a couple of hours of "sitting tight", Nicholas said, "Pull this bloody van over right now, or they'll be consequences," (So British.) Mike acted as if he didn't hear a word. I was amused.

At that point our suspicions were confirmed. There was no doubt in our minds that Mike and Jillian were trafficking hashish, and that Jenny and the rest of us were their cover. Every time the van and Mike disappeared, to return hours later, telling us that the van needed servicing. It was obvious what was going on when Mike got so crazed when he had to make his "connections."

We devised a distraction to get Mike from behind the wheel.

Madelene was sitting directly behind the driver's seat where it was easy to lean right over the drivers shoulder. She pretended to be carsick, and leaned over Mike with her face right next to his ear and said, in a real pitiful voice, "Oh God Mike, I think I'm going to barf," as she leaned over his shoulder.

Mike jammed on the brakes and flew out of the van stomping up and down, cursing, "Bloody Hell, Crikey, Fuck!" His face was blood red and he was totally out of control. By that time, six foot five James and six foot four Nicholas were out of the van and Nicholas had picked little Mike up under his arms, while he dangled in space with his short legs running nowhere.

James took over the driving and Nicholas pushed Mike down behind the drivers seat and wedged him in, almost sitting on him. Nicholas placed his arm behind Mike's neck just in case he tried anything. After we all took a bladder break, then got on our way, we were feeling quite proud of ourselves because we "pulled it off."

We captured the deranged madman who was kidnapping us. At that point Mike gave out a long sigh then put his head on Nicholas's shoulder and went fast to sleep. Mike snored, and we laughed. He was one tired little Bandito. I actually felt sorry for him.

As we drove through the night, we were hoping that the worst was over. All we wanted was to get home in one piece. I was feeling like Dorothy in The Wizard of Oz, just trying to get home to Kansas.

I have no idea of the name of the small mysterious town we stopped at in the middle of the night. There was "no room at the inn," so we were offered the roof to bed down for the night for a small fee.

As we were opening our sleeping bags and settling in; two policemen came onto the roof. They looked around at all of us without a word. One policeman saw James and asked about the hard suitcase at his feet. Reluctantly, James said, "This is my photographic equipment."

"Open it" one said. "Now hand it to me." By this time James' face was as red as the sparse hair on his head and his full beard. James was enraged.

The policeman made him take every lens, lens cap, light meter, distance gauge, cable, cleaning cloth and the packing material out of their compartments. They took their sweet time inspecting everything, then, handing it back to James. The rest of us just looked on like figures in Madame Tussaud's Wax Museum.

Without another word, the surly policemen left the roof. James' girlfriend Amanda touched his arm in a soothing gesture because she knew his pot was about to boil over; and it did. He said, "Those fucking wogs," then mumbled something under his breath.

Everyone except me seemed stunned at

James' outburst, because I was the only one who didn't realize that the reference to the word "wog" in the context it was used, was a racial slur similar to the word "nigger;" the racial slur directed at Blacks in America and Africa as well as other countries in the east, where some Arabs are referred to as "sand niggers."

Amanda was as tiny (maybe 5 feet, but shapely) as James was tall. She looked Latin with big dark eyes, black hair and an olive complexion. It was obvious that she was James' subordinate in their relationship and she accepted that position. They were both schoolteachers and very much a couple, sometimes to the exclusion of the rest of us.

As we continued to organize our gear and prepared to sleep, or not, I noticed that one-by-one, my mates quietly approached James with whispered reprimands to him. Samantha said, "I think he should apologize to you." I said, "Oh please no, if he wants to apologize to the two police officers, and disappear from the face of the earth, that's OK with me. But, I don't want his apology. I'd rather he remain embarrassed and un-forgiven so I can enjoy my silent retribution." Then, I whispered to Samantha, "He'd better watch his back and move away from the edge of the roof!" As we both looked over at James, we were laughing long and hard, but he was not.

MENAGE A TROIS, IN SPAIN

It was wonderful being in Spain again. Our "mates" stayed at the same campsite we had stopped at on our way to Morocco. It was quite decent compared to some of the campsites and rooftops we had slept on. This campsite had warm showers and clean bathrooms, what more could we ask for.

We arrived in Spain totally exhausted. By that time, my new best friend, Samantha, could hardly walk. The trip was too much of an undertaking for someone who had undergone back surgery as a result of bone cancer, just five months before. I wasn't doing so great either: my stomach was still "dubious". Nicholas was the only one with any money left, so he decided to get a hotel room for the three of us, but mostly for Samantha.

We stood on either side of her with one of our arms around her waist with each one of her arms over our shoulders, to help her walk. Even though she was in real pain, she was laughing at us being in yet another awkward situation. I said to Samantha, "people are watching us, they probably think we're two drunken whores and Nicholas is our pimp." It was hard to keep a straight face as we approached the front desk.

In his perfect English Gentleman dialect Nicholas said, "We would like a room with the largest bed you have, please."

"One room, one bed, sir?" asked the desk

clerk. "Please, if you will".

"And the ladies?"

"Oh they're with me."

As the befuddled desk clerk handed Nicholas the keys, with a slight gleam in his eyes, he said, "Enjoy your stay."

Nicholas replied with a salacious smile, "I'm sure I will."

As we entered our beautiful bright room, and checked out the incredible bathroom, we just looked at each other grinning from ear to ear. Nicholas said, "Ah civilization." We gently deposited Samantha on the bed and took her sandals off. She said, "Thank you ever-so-much, Nicholas, you are such a dear."

After Nicholas and I took our showers and changed into clean shorts and t-shirts, we put Samantha in a chair then lifted her into the bathroom; I then helped her with a nice soapy sponge bath and a change of clothes; there was no way she could get into a shower or a tub.

By this time Samantha and I were already family, and now we had Nicholas. He was with the British Diplomatic Corps, and quite well spoken. I was impressed by how un-spoiled and down-to-earth he was to be so handsome and, seemingly well off. He had a generous heart and we had come to adore him.

Nicholas was planning to go out to get us some snacks and cold beer, but we couldn't tear ourselves away from such a peaceful moment. After we all lay down in our gigantic bed and felt the softness on our weary bodies, we sighed like three old women, and had to laugh at ourselves. Samantha was on one side of the bed, Nicholas was in the middle and I was on the other side, near the bathroom.

As we reflected on the day's events, Nicholas started to laugh hysterically. He said, "Did you see that poor bloke's face when we signed in?"

"But it got worse when you asked for one room with one big bed," Samantha giggled.

I said, "Did you see that sneaky little smile on his face when he said, "Enjoy your stay," and Nicholas answered like he was the King of England, "I'm sure I will."

"We must have been quite a spectacle," Samantha said.

Nicholas said, "I'm sure the desk clerk and everyone else in the lobby thinks I'm up here having one grand old Menage a trois, and here I am with a lovely blond who can't walk and a gorgeous "exotic" who's got the trots; some bloody Menage a trois this is!"

There was a knock on our door; it was Sam, our eighteen-year old travel mate. He was a sweet country boy on his maiden voyage. We all basked in his innocent delight at everything. He was excited about different foods, the change of scenery and traveling by van, hovercraft and ferry. To him Morocco was such a different world from anything he knew. He was in awe at everything.

Sam was a friendly boy who hadn't traveled much outside of his hometown, where his family had a farm. He was lanky kid with longish brown hair and a ready smile. He had a thick cockney accent I couldn't get enough of. I harassed him to no end, just to make him respond to me.

We liked him right away. The teachers in our group took pleasure in introducing him to the many wonders of the world. We watched him fall in love with everything new and exciting.

He came to bid us farewell because he was leaving our group to join an Italian family he had met at the beach that day; serendipity. Sam spent the day with them, eating, talking, and playing with the younger children and their teen-aged brother. The family was obviously charmed by Sam, and invited him to join them on the rest of their voyage as they headed back to Italy in their trailer.

Sam was a great kid. We hugged and kissed him goodbye, and Nicholas slipped him some money (like a favorite uncle). Sam seemed to "Walk in the light" and good fortune followed him.

After bidding Sam farewell, we three were ready for some well-earned sleep. Nicholas asked, "Are you alright Love, need anything?" Samantha replied sleepily, "No, thank you, I'm just splendid." Regardless of her pain or discomfort, she was always positive and very brave. Then he then turned to me and asked if I needed anything, and I said, "Besides being here with my new best friend and a big handsome bloke beside me in bed, the only other thing I could use is one damn big box of money so we can all do this again, in style."

I got hit with pillows and we laughed and laughed. I realized what a precious moment in time this was for us, and I knew that I would carry it in my heart, always.

BEHAVING BADLY

After encountering so many unexpected circumstances beyond our control, that had to be handled with the utmost diplomacy during our Moroccan voyage, there were still more un-welcomed surprises the gods had in store for us.

By the time we reached the hovercraft in Calais, France, We were like soldiers with battle fatigue. Since we were unwillingly whisked through the wilds of Morocco, passing those colorful markets beaconing us, we had no time to shop.

At that point we just wanted to get back to England and away from what had turned into a nightmare. All we wanted was to take a later hovercraft so we could do some shopping at the departure port; even though we only had enough money left for some cheap trinkets and souvenirs. When we told Mike our intentions, he said, "You all can do what you damn well please but I'm getting on that hovercraft, now."

The heavy connecting chains had already been removed from the dock in preparation for departure when we realized that Mike still had our passports. He usually held on to them to be presented at the many checkpoints we passed through. We hadn't gotten them back. Once again we were held hostage by trust and stupidity.

We called out to the few crewmembers at the rear of the craft, "Wait, wait, please, wait for us, he's got our passports and all of our luggage is on the van!" There were too many of us running towards the dock screaming, to be ignored. We jumped on the craft just in time.

As we (ladies) looked for available seats, without any warning James and Nicholas approached Mike, snatched him from his seat and proceeded to beat the hell out of him. Poor little Mike was cursing and begging, while trying to ward off the blows being wielded by the two giants. Mike was on his knees in the isle thrashing around. Those two gentlemen, James and Nicholas had finally been pushed completely "Over the edge."

Some of the crew arrived and stopped the fight. Mike continued his vulgar tirade and a steward threatened to "Get the authorities." We were all a little hysterical, shouting, "He's got our passports and is trying to steal our luggage! He's been holding us hostage for weeks," we whined.

It must have appeared rather ridiculous to our spectators, looking at one crazy little guy being subdued by the crew, compared to the two dudes, both over six feet tall, "doing him in." Even we "ladies" were bigger than Mike.

Someone who looked like he was in charge, (probably the captain) intervened and shouted, "Quiet, or I'll put the lot of you off this craft."

He addressed Mike first, "Do you have their

passports?"

"Yes sir", he answered pitifully.

"Give them back to them, immediately."

"Right."

"Are you in possession of their belongings?"

"Yes sir, in the van, sir."

"Do you intend to return them to their proper owners, or do I need to call ahead to Dover to have you detained when you arrive?"

"Yes sir, I mean no sir, please don't do that, I'll give them all their stuff, sir."

"Now all of you sit down so we can be on our way, God willing. And you call yourselves adults?"

We skimmed the ocean in absolute silence for sometime trying to come down from all of the latest hysteria. Then I whispered to the ladies, "How embarrassing, I hope my kids don't hear about this." We tried not to laugh too loud but couldn't help ourselves. Then Fanny said, "You couldn't even see him under those two big blokes, I thought it was a bit much. I could have done it without even hurting him, poor little guy." That did it, we were "off again."

"It was awful, did they beat him badly?"

asked sweet Madelene, who wouldn't hurt a fly.

"I don't think so, just some scratches and a bloody nose." Frances chimed in.

Samantha said, "It could have been much worse, seems like they were holding back, they could have really hurt him if they wanted to."

We were all behaving so badly, everyone was looking at us, I was mortified, and I didn't want to be "The Ugly American" on the trip.

Then our "wild card", Frances said, "I don't know about the rest of you but, I'm having the time of my life!"

HIJACKED

When we finally arrived at the port in Dover, before we could even get out of the van to kiss the ground, Mike jumped out of the van, grabbed Jenny's hand as they ran to the customs building, looking for a telephone, we assumed. Mike was in such a panic, we were sure he was trying to make his "connection." Or had missed it.

We stretched our legs while waiting for Mike to return. Then Jenny came back to the van. She was in a very playful mood. She said, "Dad said he's going to leave you all here, but it's a secret game, so don't tell." She put her finger on her lips, giggled, and ran back to the building.

I don't know why anyone was surprised. The storm was not over yet. We all had the same thought at the same time. Jillian just shook her head and said, "Come on, I'll drive, he's gone completely mad, I'm so sorry." We took the van and headed for London: home.

We were at Nicholas's flat, sprawled out on the colorful rug in his small living room, drinking wine and reflecting on all of the craziness we endured. As we wallowed in the pleasure of our survival, there was a knock on the door.

There stood two "bobbies", obviously looking for us, the hijackers.

"Won't you come in?" said Nicholas, the perfect gentleman. The merry-making stopped immediately, as we all sat at attention.

The "bobbies" came into the living room and said "Good afternoon." We were speechless. "We understand that you've all just arrived from a tour to Morocco, is that right," one of them asked.

We replied, "Yes sir."

"May I have your names and your passports please? It seems like Mr. Michael Wikam filed a complaint against the lot of you for taking his vehicle without his permission, is that so?"

"I had permission, sir," answered Jillian in her most proper Queens' English, "I am the co-host of the Moroccan tour and Michael and I share the driving and the responsibility for the vehicle. He and I were having a personal disagreement, which has nothing to do with these people. He has a nasty temper, so I thought it best for us to distance ourselves from him. We've all had a taste of his terrible temper, at times putting us in danger, so I suggested that we leave him at the port to find other transportation."

"Damn she's smooth" I whispered to someone near me. I was very impressed with Jillian's panache and calm under fire. I thought to myself, "I bet she's the brains behind this whole caper."

One of the officers said, "Well, alright then, we'll see what Mr. Wikam plans to do about his complaint."

I said, "Officer, if actual charges are

brought against us, will I have to appear in court?"

"Most likely."

"But I'm booked on a ship to New York in a couple of weeks."

"Well if that happens, then you'll have to stay, won't you."

"I can't stay, I'm out of money and my hosts in Buckinghamshire are going on vacation the day after I leave!" I was in a panic.

"Seems like you might have some decisions to make, doesn't it," said the other officer.

I was in such a state by then that I didn't realize that the officers were just, "having some fun with me"

They said, "Good day", then left.

Everyone was having a good laugh at my expense. I said, "What the hell is so funny?"

Nicholas said, "You must know by now that Mike is just mucking us about. He knows that if he brings charges against us we'll have him investigated for drug smuggling; besides, our lovely Jillian here just put the last nail in Mike's coffin by telling the "bobbies" that he has already endangered us all by driving while insane. You're fine, not to worry." He filled my wine glass again while I exhaled.

FAREWELL

For better or worse we all came away from our Moroccan adventure forever changed. We, (the British, Welsh, Australian and American) came together and became family, if only for a little while, sharing a "Once in a lifetime" experience. We took a chance and rose above the many obstacles placed in our path, and survived, almost unscathed.

As we all sat around mellowed by wine, reflecting on our great adventure, Samantha said, "I wouldn't have missed this for anything."

"I wouldn't have either."

Sometime around 1981, my sister, Marge and I went to Wales to visit Samantha's family and put a conch shell from St. Croix on her grave, so that she could hear the ocean.

-- Marcia Jameson

Don Cox

Eternal Life

A small red squirrel, sick and miserable, awaits oblivion in the warmth of a broad stretch of gravel road in a remote corner of Nova Scotia. When the fever passes and he is once again aware of his surroundings, he finds himself nestled in the pocket of a corduroy shirt (St. Mary's blue in color), worn by a red-bearded young man riding in the passenger seat of a 1960 Jeep FC170 pickup truck. The truck has the name "Mar-a-nath-a" stenciled on its sides; and the driver is a woman whom our hero soon discovers to have a considerable sympathy for unhappy squirrels.

"Mar-a-nath-a" is Aramaic, but by a strange quirk of fate, it can be found in better English dictionaries. By an even stranger quirk, Aramaic is the native tongue of Nova Scotian red squirrels. So our small friend is aware that one possible translation is "The Lord has come." He concludes that he has died and is in transit to heaven, a place well known among the cognoscenti to have an abundance of hickory nuts, and where it is never winter when one needs to pee. So he settles back in comfort to await his destiny, escorted by his guardian angels.

Five thousand miles of the Trans Canadian highway to Vancouver, British Columbia and fifteen hundred miles of the Pacific Coast Highway from there to San Diego, California pass beneath their wheels.

Apparently, heaven is located just north of San Diego because that is where they set up housekeeping, in an upstairs apartment. As foretold, their mansion has many rooms, but the squirrel is surprised at having to chew holes at the bottoms of the doors in order to move freely from one room to another. He is particularly intrigued that his angels keep boarding up the holes, so he keeps having to make new ones. He supposes, though, that it is just some sort of celestial exercise program and participates with gusto.

Also as anticipated, hickory nuts abound. At four each morning he gnaws voraciously on them, scattering the shells widely about. The angels seem to be cranky about all the early morning racket, but this being heaven, he knows they must be kidding, and he continues his ritual, unfazed by their complaints.

And best of all, there is no winter. When he needs to relieve himself, he does so in complete comfort on the upper edges of the many books he finds conveniently placed on the shelves in his spacious bedroom.

All seems to be well, but within a few weeks he begins to feel that something is missing, perhaps more than one something.

Finally, at Christmastime he is given a tree to play in. A tree! Wow! And he races up its slender trunk and out onto a branch in sudden ecstasy. Once there however, he is seized by an overwhelming passion, grabs the branch end, bends it around and bites off the tip. He then rushes in a frenzy to the ends of each of the other branches, until he has eaten all the tips. What he and his guardian angels had not realized, apparently, was that he had an enormous need for greens, something always before so abundant and ordinary that he had not appreciated them.

Greens are thereafter supplied, in addition to the hickory nuts and water, but the tree soon dries up and is taken away. With that, his good spirits founder and our little friend enters a period of depression. Heaven is OK, as far as it goes, but it just doesn't quite satisfy the spiritual needs of a once free-range squirrel from the magnificence that is Nova Scotia.

A day comes when he is tricked into a box and carried out of the apartment. Soon they are on the road again. Concerned that his lack of gratitude for the bounty of heaven might have set him on the road to hell, he chews his way out of the box when no one is looking. This time he finds himself in a sleek 1956 Studebaker coupe, heading north.

The car stops after a couple of hours, at a house in the La Habra hills. Fearing what lies ahead, he hides under the driver's seat, up inside the springs where he can't be found.

When the angels discover that he has escaped, they search frantically, but eventually have to admit defeat, and walk away, leaving the car doors open to indicate that he is free to leave.

Later, when he feels the coast is clear, our

anxious little friend pops out to have a look around. He soon realizes that the gray squirrels of Nova Scotia, whose religion he had once mocked, might actually have been correct in some small way. This new location is surely the true heaven, with freedom, trees galore, still no winter, and things the like of which he'd never dreamed: apricots, avocados, limes, wonders everywhere, and no more of those infernal hickory nuts. Apparently his previous location had been in purgatory, where he had been forced to confront his true needs. The gray squirrels had said that would happen, but he hadn't believed them.

During his months in San Diego, he had grown somewhat attached to human company, without quite realizing it; the angels had seemed such a nuisance most of the time, even though they clearly adored him. But here in the true heaven, even good company is available, in moderate and controllable doses. Whenever he likes, he can amuse himself of a morning by appearing on the bedroom windowsill of the house on the hill, to be admired and pampered by the strange old woman who lives there. (The young couple with the Studebaker had left the scene the day after his escape. He'd overheard them saying something about the approach of a fearsome monster they'd mentioned on other occasions, "Monday," they called it. Anyway, they left, vowing to approach the monster once again with courage, and to do fair battle. He felt sorry for them, and at their departure, but only briefly. His job, he felt, was to show proper appreciation for the heaven they'd delivered him to.)

So our plucky little Nova Scotian has found heaven, or maybe Eden, and is settling in to enjoy like hell his eternal life. And enjoy he does, for long days and joyous nights, in the process lighting up the life of the old woman when he appears at her window for their morning chat.

But, because he had been unwilling to listen to the wisdom of the gray squirrels of his youth, even making fun of their religion, they hadn't bothered to inform him that according to their careful calculations, eternity is actually only six days long (the same as the period of creation, a situation they referred to as "equipartition").

So he is totally surprised when on his sixth day in the hills, while scampering across the roof of the old woman's house, he is snatched aloft by a hawk for one last brief excursion.

Very likely he would have taken little consolation from the fact that he was then to be mourned for many months by the young couple and the old woman whose hearts he had so easily and totally captured.

-- Don Cox

Don Cox

The Brownie Hawkeye Christmas

I was a peculiar kid who grew into a similarly peculiar adult -- thanks perhaps to the influences of some of the women in my family. My awareness of this began on one particular Christmas day between dinner and dessert, in the kitchen with Mom, Grandma, and my aunt. The men folk were elsewhere, goofing around or snoozing on couches here and there. (I had a new Kodak Brownie Hawkeye camera and still have photographic proof of this being The Way Things Were.)

After shooting up my roll of film, I fell into one of my funny moods. It was during a phase in which I was becoming less and less certain I knew what everything was about, a situation I found unsettling. At some point my mother noticed that I seemed to be hanging about the kitchen door, moping. She invited me into the kitchen where everything was light and action, and after a moment told me she thought it was time I heard her version of the Cinderella story -- a treatise on the layers of truth.

She sat us down at the table and focused her mind in a way that I had previously seen only when she was preparing to reassemble a little wooden puzzle that had been her father's and she had mastered as a child. (I say reassemble because this occurred from time to time when I brought the pieces to her after having once again taken the puzzle apart, and failed again to get it back together.) When she was ready, she told her peculiar story the same way she assembled the puzzle, precisely and from memory.

I was about 12 that Christmas, and found the story's sexuality callous and embarrassing. In preparing to write this, I went through her papers which now, unhappily, live in a box in my attic, and found a typed copy of her story dated 1927. I could not believe that the Mom I knew had written it when she was only 16! But she wasn't yet that woman, was still assembling the bits and pieces of the one she would become.

Anyway, I reproduce it here, though not from memory, a commodity that I did not inherit.

Cinderella's Innocence
A.B.C. 1927

Things, apparently, are never quite as they seem.

The fabled glass slipper, for example, was actually silver, fashioned by a castle smith at the Prince's request. And initially it was quite small.

As his search progressed, the charming prince was gracious enough to spend a few weeks at a seacoast villa with each of the maidens whose foot seemed to fit the shoe. But then at night he gently worked the metal on an anvil, and the shoe gradually expanded to fit no longer. In time he worked his way through all the starry-eyed damsels of his realm, from small foot to large.

There was in this land one woman who recognized the deceit and earned for herself three separate occasions at the villa, using various folk arts to influence her foot size over the course of years. On the third occasion, she seemed familiar to the Prince, who, having tired somewhat of his amusement, mistook this familiarity for the resonance of love, and proposed marriage.

After they were wed, the Prince had quite a surprise. The new Princess it turned out, was egalitarian, a populist with a terrible distaste for royalist behavior. She had snared the Prince in that long ago land only to gain access to his mother's library, the finest one around.

My grandma (my father's mother) had been listening carefully to Mom's recitation and claimed at the end that she had never heard it before. She also seemed to get quite a chuckle out of the story (another hint that I really had very little idea what these women were about.)

Apparently Mom's example put her in a sharing mood, as Grandma then said she'd decided it was time she let me in on a useful secret too, and got her Bible from the next room. Opening it to Psalms, she took out a plastic laminated sheet of paper and showed me her version of the 23rd Psalm -- in praise of the protective power of the subjunctive mood. I was not yet old enough to appreciate the import of its message, but I was sure as heck surprised to be shown this by a woman who'd for years made sure I got to Methodist Sunday school almost every week. Because she later gave me a dramatic cross-stitch wall hanging of her psalm for my birthday, a token that I have never lost, I can again provide you with the exact text.

MASTERY OVER DOUBT: JANUS 23

Yea though I walk through the
valley of the shadow of doubt,
I will fear no error;
for thy "might" is with me;
thy "would" and thy "should"
they comfort me.
Thou preparest a table before me
in the presence of my
uncertainties;
thou salvest my head from roil;
my cup runneth over.

Surely "Acceptance is Mastery" shall
follow me through all the
doubts of my life;
and I shall dwell in the house of
Subjunctive,
forever.

It would be a long time before I was comfortable with the layers of truth in my mother's story, and proficient in the use of the protective powers of subjunctive (or maybe it's more accurately the Conditional Mood) advertised by my grandmother. But I'd at least had the notions inserted into my brain and I felt (rather than understood) their power. Apart from that, I was mainly uneasy. These women, however, appeared to be having an awfully good time, either with me or at my expense.

I was totally unaware then that as an adult I would discover my aunt's profound honesty, good sense, and caring nature. As a child I had always thought of her as a rather severe woman, so I did not realize, that Christmas, that she sensed the strength of my turbulence and sought to calm me, while taking her turn at me and making yet a third point.

She seemed to change the subject, asking me about what I was learning in math at school. She soon guided the conversation to the two strange numbers, "π" and "e", that she remembered from her days in school, long before. She said she remembered hearing that these numbers are known to umpteen decimal places, and that they are also known to go on forever. Then she took a yardstick out of the broom closet and a sugar jar off a corner shelf. She said something like, "Look, the diameter of the lid of this jar is about 4 and (2.5)/8ths inches, uh, 4 and 5/16ths I guess." I noticed that she placed the 1 inch mark on the left edge of the lid and then had subtracted an inch from the reading on the other side. It seemed an unnecessary complication, and I asked about it. She said it was a habit she'd developed sewing, "Yardsticks are funny. You can never be sure the end is where zero ought to be, so I always measure from 1 and subtract." Then she took a piece of string from a drawer, wrapped it around the edge of the lid and used a pen to mark where the string met itself after going once around the lid. "These two points on the string are one circumference apart, wouldn't you say?" Using the yardstick to measure the string, which turned out to be slightly elastic, she continued, "So, the circumference is, somewhere between 13 and 3/8ths and 13 and 7/8ths inches, depending on how tightly I pulled the string before marking it. So, what is the value of π from this measurement?"

Believe it or not, we didn't have calculators or computers in those days. And she wouldn't tell me what the point of this exercise was, until I'd gone off and divided the circumference by the diameter, using long division (after converting everything to 16ths of an inch) and come back with the answer. Meanwhile those three went mirthfully back to getting some of the dishes cleaned up and dessert ready.

I chased down paper and pen and eventually found π to lie between about 3.10 and 3.22. Having watched the measurement, I was sure she'd pulled the string a lot harder for the second measurement on the yardstick than she had on the lid. So I thought the answer should have been closer to the smaller value, though there was the problem of avoiding the thread grooves in the metal lid. Results in hand, I then stood by the door to the kitchen waiting to be noticed. It took a while, but finally she came over to see what I'd gotten, and I got my chance to ask what the point was.

On noticing that the range of her uncertainty was large, she remarked, "Well, that was a very quick measurement. I could do a lot better, and those people at the Bureau of Standards, I'm sure, could do much better yet, though maybe not on Christmas Day while getting dessert. But no one is ever going to measure π to the umpteen decimal places that the experts tell us it is known, or the infinite number of decimal places they say it could be known if we had time and inclination to take up the chase. How do they know all those decimal places, and why should we believe them when they say they do?"

I don't recall reacting immediately to this query, and if I didn't for real, I would give myself a fair amount of credit for progress even at that point. She didn't want an answer; she wanted me to think about the question, and to think a good long time.

I could tell that Grandma was chuckling again, even though she had her back turned. I recalled having been told that in her younger years she'd taught school in a one room schoolhouse in Yuma, Arizona. I think that was before my dad was bitten by the rattlesnake and almost lost his leg, before they moved to Compton, California and he became a star of track and football, before I didn't get those genes either. Funny what things'll jump into your brain if you let them. Already I wasn't thinking about the problem, until my aunt spoke again.

"And what about "e"? There isn't even something to measure to find out how big it is. They claim it's just a handy base or something for logs." And then, with a perfectly straight face, "Maybe if we could find out what it is, we could stack firewood on it. In fact, that's just what we'll do. You go figure out what "e" is, not from what 'they' say, but all by yourself, and next Christmas come tell me the answer. Maybe we can find some good use for it."

I think that was the only time I ever saw her wink. "But now some pie of a different sort," as she plunked a beauty of a pumpkin pie on the pullout cutting board and bisected it four times into eight almost perfectly equal-sized pieces. "Donnie, why don't you go tell Ellen and the boys to get washed up for dessert?" I understood she meant 'boys' to include my uncle and father besides my male cousins and brother. "Wait a moment," commanded Mom, "I could use a hug." But I knew it was for me, and that somehow I'd found my way into a sorority, or maybe a coven, of which I'd previously been totally unaware.

I recently saw a bumper sticker that very nicely summarized a big part of my aunt's message. It read:

Apart from that, I've decided not to try here to translate these three messages, or to pontificate on them.

I do recommend that you review them from time to time through the accumulation of your life experience. See whether they aren't suggesting you take less rigid positions, or coaxing you into deeper perspective with a broader view of what might possibly be occurring, or giving you the true courage required for <u>lack</u> of conviction, or suggesting that you ground your perception in independent evaluation and understanding. For me, their review has repeatedly proven to be useful.

Oh, by the way, if you want to make a great pumpkin pie, try putting sesame seeds in the pie pan before putting in the crust. Also, for a little variety, mix some shredded coconut into the custard, getting it good and wetted so it doesn't singe where it sticks out the top.

-- Don Cox

My Love Affair

At first, I resisted the spontaneous embrace and immediate call for engagement, although I expected a response to my invitation. I sought to make an impression with a fresh, optimistic outlook and joyful colors, and based on past disappointments, was wishing for any reception that would rate above passive indulgence. But I had a gnawing sense that in return, something inexplicit was being asked of me.

In my search for reliable support I was advised to focus on compatibility this time around. Actually, more intercourse was also recommended; but upon hearing that word, the novice English speaker that I was couldn't fully comprehend how the advice applied to my situation, or what exactly would ensue if I were to follow it. The only thought I could allow myself at the time was that a higher degree of interaction was necessary, so I was prepared to show flexibility in that exercise.

I also believed that I was capable of adapting my stance to any circumstance, even though it turned out to be more a function of my own self-serving understanding of how river flowed over stone. In reality, I disliked the idea of dictating the course of action as much as relinquishing the commanding role.

Early on, I detected and underestimated a quiet eagerness coupled with a deceptive appearance of fragility. What I perceived as sincere but conditional acceptance was distracting and enervating because I didn't care for the give and take of a demanding exchange. Too often, in the aftermath of our encounters, when all wetness had dried up, I watched the joy fade out of my bright colors, sucked up by an insatiable, but kindred being, amazingly athirst for my lavish washes. I was the artist, groomed to master the medium; but paper, always fully present yet soft and delicate, responded so compellingly to my advances, setting the pace of interaction, suggesting deeper and more sustained relationship. Nothing unfolded as I anticipated, as I desired, and my game plan went awry at every turn.

All I needed was the right surface to paint on, one that would be more suitable for wet techniques. Paper was suggested because, given my natural inclination toward fluidity, *"a porous surface would be an ideal complement,"* I was told, *"acid-free paper, one-hundred-percent rag, beautiful surface quality,"* certified my art supplier, and I was enthusiastic about the prospect of serious experimentation with a material less neutral than canvas.

I was an enchantress, and the magic I made relied mostly on newly acquired knowledge and skills. I was schooled in the art of fostering illusion, a sleight of hand, deliberate and sure. I was aware of my mission and abilities, and the material I purchased was mine to use as I pleased for casting spells, unadulterated by outside influence, certainly not the result of transaction with art paraphernalia or the vagaries of oversensitive fibers that, in their own fashion, also had their way with water. The tension lent an air of competition to our exchange, when there should have been no doubt as to who would get to shape the outcome of my efforts. After all, to the magician that I was, this matter was one of artisanship and practicality, the lesser parts in my act of creation.

Along with a dream to pursue, I also had a specific problem to solve: I needed a safe place to deliver the wet marks of over-diluted paint that my annoyed oil painting instructor complained didn't do justice to an impermeable medium. I barely received a passing grade in his class for not being sufficiently "painterly", unwilling to apply generous layers of smooth and creamy oil paint on bare canvas.

My shortcomings with the oil medium stemmed from the fact that I had a propensity for tinting a surface when painting, and canvas had no use for the abundance of fluid I insisted on using. Once the excess solvent had evaporated, it was obvious that my transparent and runny colors did not impress the impenetrable surface against which they appeared anemic. In retrospect, I think that I was repulsed by the toxic smell of turpentine and, until today, I prefer to *achieve* white, bobbing and weaving along with the changes and fluctuations occurring in the natural whiteness of paper, creating light from within, rather than spreading milky paint from a tube on a totally lifeless canvas.

That tendency appeared already to be the sign of a pronounced artistic temperament and the reason why I gravitated toward water media. But I had prematurely put a picture in my mind, one with the hard edge of something I thought I knew. I was ready to "fly" into the world of picture-making, and a false sense of clarity led me to assume that the rest was as automatic as identifying the appropriate surface on which my own fixed desires could play. Paper supported me in my shortsighted attempts, but in its own way, offering itself, taking me in on its own terms while also humbling and frustrating me.

Only when I was finally willing to abandon my immature agenda, to let go of my well-ordered plot, preconceived roadmap and undigested art instructions, only when I became secure enough to simply let my intuition guide me to the elements of paper that called to me, only then did my failures and mishaps become my manner.

On my page, excessive fluidity and unconditional absorbency eventually recognized each other as soon as my head and my nerves got out of the way. My teacher's assessment and advice would prove to be well founded: I was born to work on paper. We were made for each other and will bring the best out of one another. More importantly, I saw my conflicted self reflected back in paper's view of me: my medium of choice will actually conspire to expose my lack of self-knowledge.

Paper and I were no strangers to each other, so it is ironic that the idea and decision to reach for it at that point in my life came as a recommendation from a tutor. Like most children, I discovered the pleasures of artistic expression and my ability to draw in casual trials with crayons and paper. It was known in my family that my favorite birthday gifts were art books and supplies and, one memorable day, my mother surprised me with a watercolor box and pads that I had eyed for two years at the *Librairie Deschamp* in town.

If I could only recapture that time of playful awe and fascination when I was blissfully ignorant of rules and only my senses -eyes, sight, touch - were engaged in the process of creation. How I wish I had preserved the aquarelles of my childhood when I was mesmerized, not unsettled, by the random effects of watercolor on paper. I retained no memory of the pictures themselves or anything about their execution, but I can recall painting with abandon, and I never really forgot the freedom and joy of water painting.

But I grew up, traveled, envisioned art as a career and attended school where I was taught art theory and how to paint in a conventional manner. It took a gaucherie on canvas to make me aware of my loss of artistic naïveté, and the fact that it couldn't be recaptured by force of will.

I had already taken the path towards indoctrination, so I had no other choice than to stay the course, hoping that at the end of that path I could move beyond the mental alteration and proceed, in a manner that was right for me, with what happened to be a fortuitous reacquaintance with an old love.

The training I received contributed valuable knowledge and improved craftsmanship. I was coached on how to compensate for the rapid drying, mitigate the loss of water and its draining effect on pigments. I even practiced immersing pages in a tub of water for hours in order to pre-empt shrinkage before usage. However, my technical instruction amounted, in general, to what I saw as more tricks to control watercolor in order to suit my intention. I could excel at containing the effluence of the medium to the point of removing all visible signs of water in tight detailed paintings but, for reasons I will understand later, something in me went against that game of conquest and confrontation.

My reluctance to use these moves and countermoves was due to the fact that I didn't want to work against paper, attempting ineffectually to quell what I perceived as a watery onslaught that restricted my creative movement. Besides, the resulting ill-conceived washes seemed to rinse away the memory that I so desperately needed to rekindle.

Time spent plying the craft in self-education, more hands-on familiarity with the materials, and above all, the courage to examine my resistance and perceived failure would pay off. I flooded paper with water, over and over, and helplessly watched my perfect compositional schemes slip away, out of order, until I realized that happy accidents were happening on the page, awakening in me an innate sense of adventure and a childhood feeling of visual wonderment.

The notion occurred to me that I could let go of learned methods and work in unison with water and paper. That's when I adjusted my attitude and decided to wipe my mind clear of borrowed formulas in order to undertake what Gauguin called "painting without recipes," I made it a practice to revisit painting as a wide-eyed girl from Haiti, free to let her imaginative mind roam, prompt to be excited about a promising voyage while unsure of the destination.

"Don't sweat over a painting" wrote Gauguin, "a great sentiment can be rendered immediately.

Dream on it and look for the simplest form in which you can express it..." I knew that paper was suggesting to me the way to realize my dream and arrive at that simplest form: to stop going against the flow, to allow chance to play a role in my painting process, to honor the part of me that longed to paint with total freedom, that the time was right to meet with the unintended.

Paper brought me the message that such approach could be instructive, as if it was able to remember before I could the shared moments of my early creative life, a time I want to remain forever present in my memory. That breakthrough led to a totally new direction in my artistic life and our bond grew closer. I committed to a way of painting that honored an innate wisdom that came from within my mind with an unlimited and conscious approach to an activity I was once taught.

The adoption of a preferred medium in one's artistic life is a personal and subjective decision, comparable to choosing a companion for a lasting relationship. Those who become oil painters usually start with that decision and, as a consequence, recognize canvas to be the best support. In my case, I had no preference at the time of my reunion with paper, only a predicament following my failed experiment with canvas. When I opted for careerism and a new nationality, I seemed to have distanced myself from memories that could have informed my option by incorporating childhood passions into the process. So my artistic evolution took a more empirical course.

In a sense, the decision was facilitated by the incompatibility between my natural disposition and the tuition I had received so far. Without my dilemma, I wonder what kind of artist I would have been. I instinctively rejected the "doormat" personality of canvas and found the sponge-like personality of paper to be more attractive, although it presented many drawbacks at the time. But embracing paper came with the basic challenge to overcome the elements in the process of water painting that caused me to create in a reactive mode.

The truth is that the exploratory nature of my work was better served by a medium that heightened my alertness to the support, which in turn heightened the act of seeing and knowing. Besides, I was motivated by the promise of all that I could learn about myself if I were to take stock of the mental habits underlying my aversion to canvas and my conflicts with paper.

A cloth initially, canvas is primed, rendered waterproof before usage so, unlike paper, it doesn't "talk back" and is ideal for a unilateral posture in painting. Oil paints offer the benefit of a slower pace of drying, which allows for leisurely applications of juicy impastos, the kind which would have gained the approbation of my teacher. The maker can scrape paint off the very rugged surface, manipulate his composition, paint over it and change his mind indefinitely. The art created on canvas is also considered more serious, durable, and valuable, guaranteed to last thousands of years. So oil painting on canvas is elevated in the academic world and the oil painter benefits from the prestige of a long historic tradition.

By contrast, there is something casual and modest about paper. A work on paper is regarded as a mere sketch, a preparation for "serious" art: the stuff of tentative art work. A watercolor is classified as a drawing in museums, never reaching the level and finish of painting in the hierarchies of the arts.

However, despite the appealing cachet of canvas and the difficulties I had experienced so far in my transition efforts, I identified with paper in the most visceral way. All things considered, I was still more inclined to esteem the value I would derive personally from utilizing it. It appeared tempting, at the time, to set my expectations free and paint again with the curiosity of a child, focusing on starting more than finishing, losing myself in the activity itself with less trepidation about the end product.

I determined then that, for my artistic purpose, the main issue was one of "feedback," the very thing I welcomed with suspicion when paper offered it so spontaneously. I desired interaction, "back and forth," but I was equally intent on securing enough freedom from the craft to monitor the feelings I was encountering while painting and to let my thoughts flow through me.

I wanted the process to afford me the latitude to witness the mood stirred up by the marks I made on the page, the opportunity for reflection and even to fill my journal with musings on the creative experience. I had to devise a mode of interaction with the medium and develop the habits of mind that would permit me to be, simultaneously, adroit technically and aloft mentally.

I waited for images to emerge, unimpeded, in order to observe the whim of water and the imaginative mind at work, improvising together on the animated stage paper provided. Having accepted that my obsessive claim of control only deprived me of opportunities to extend myself, I limited my input to a light and loose gestural brushwork, simply offering, with a touch of purple, the gentle energy of an aspiration, an appeal to set miraculous happenings in motion.

I watched unfocused emotions being born into marks, marks awakening waves of thoughts, then soon, water disappearing, revealing the subtle colors of an inner monologue. I was awestruck by the resilience of transcendental images from childhood, enchantments of the past sought out by liquid paint rising up from deep within my psyche to rejoin the clear water of life. I was touched with unease about losing my habitual coolness and precision in composing a picture, but felt moved to the brink of distraction from a sense of loss that also served as an opening to amazement.

With time, I started to see past my own needs and became more attentive to paper's attributes as a painting surface, to look for manifestations of venerable qualities. I examined closely its physical substance as well as its energetic body. When paper is touched by water, sympathy unfolds seamlessly with an organic spontaneity, reminiscent of earth allowing rain to fall on it. I caught myself caressing the page like a second skin with pores, interstices, feeling the liveliness of delicate pulp that can tear at a rough touch. I began to trust it as a living entity, a being, and to appreciate it as a patient messenger and teacher.

Paper has nothing to hide or to be concealed under opaque paint. Unlike plain canvas, which has no intrinsic beauty, the delightful complexion of paper shines through a work of art, giving it incomparable luminosity. It now seems predictable that, over a period of time, I would have come to understand paper to be more than silent matter and, as a support, to mean more than an inanimate object with a passive function in my visionary endeavor.

My mind eventually caught up with the instinct that had led me all along in my search, although I am still not sure when I fully welcomed paper's active role in the mark-marking that awoke such evocative associations in me.

I gently sprayed water on its quiet face, traced a line of pure sepia ink in the dampness, and noticed that I was entering a space of limpidity in a magical face-to-face where there was no reprieve to stabilize the quivering stain made by my irresolute hand. I identified with the clarifying effect of water as I was slowly becoming what I was seeing. Did the pictures we co-created show me the way, or did my heart finally surrender to the love I was feeling?

In retrospect, it appears reasonable that in order for paper to occupy a place of honor in an artist's practice, heart and mind; in order to disregard academia's prejudices, one must be possessed with a sincere need for partnership and dialogue with a responsive medium that's awake, rich with life and always willing.

Along with these factors, the readiness to accept one's own creative findings, especially when contradictory to teachings, is essential. Additionally, the desire to learn from one's inner child requires self-trust and faith, a need to live in the light of something which has always been there.

Now that I know what paper was asking of me all along, I have come to treasure the directness and immediacy that I once found so unsettling. Soaking up my colors is simply the mark of its love, evidence of its receptiveness. I yearn to inhabit such state of spontaneity, and dare to approach the creative act alert and open, confident that it is safe to put forth an unedited stream of consciousness, and that paper will enable me in my pursuit.

I rely on that soft place to land when, from the smoke of my dreams, my unconscious thoughts lust for the purest language: a direct tongue is spoken on breathing paper with nothing lost in translation.

If undertaken from a lighthearted place of being, the task of painting, even when it stirs up dark emotions, is immensely pleasurable and transformative, capable of leading to insight, engendering the joy of discovery. I now approach paper without fear of intimacy, the defining quality of a revelatory *pas-de-deux* which reduces both of us to candor and nakedness.

I have since learned, by the way, that the word intercourse denotes many things. But harmony, I might offer by way of nuance, is what I enjoy with this favorite medium; and genuine intimacy, rather than the perfunctory execution of artwork, or the typical *mise-en-page,* dominated by its traditional accoutrements of careful placement and calculated geometries.

Favoring paper as a medium in my creative work, I became its studious apprentice, inviting its impact on my life on a larger scale, learning lessons about living by being taught the real lesson of absorbency, of openness to other, of oneness. I was ready, at last, to take to heart paper's proposal of permanent relationship, and to extend that disposition to feeling a kinship with all my materials. I became one with my helpers without concern for being steered wrong or gaining mastery over them. We all come together to bring to life beauty that would otherwise remain unborn; we are all instruments in a bigger picture, incomplete, in need of another. So my desire to work in tandem with them or to follow their own path is genuine, and our daily interplay enhances my creative life by affirming what already is.

I believe to have found the ideal support and best allies for creating true magic without tricks and calculation: a conductor with its own life force - whether it is held in anticipation in a pregnant belly of sable hair, or in the form of lightly misted moisture, a drizzle or blindly splashed ink- water carries me with its energy flow as I make my way into the unknown. My eyes and hand simply join its natural connection with color for an effortless brush dance that just happens on the page.

Painting has acquired a simplicity that makes the ritual of art making so fundamental and enlightening. And, as I lift my brush, speed and clarity come easily, and I no longer hold my breath at the moment of flight, leaving the outcome in the care of fate.

When anxiety over the volatility of watercolors rears its ugly head, I often think about a friend who dropped out of the art program at the time, and was labeled a quitter by our teacher. She later shared with me the creative experience that had changed her life while attending an art retreat at a monastery. Before painting, the class labored to make their own paper from banana leaves or other fibers and, after painting, in a sort of calling into loss, released the art work back to the environment, some by burying it, others burning or leaving it out in the rain, in order to cultivate non-attachment and practice living in the present.

What better mission for art than being an enticement to awareness? I began to challenge my assumptions and examine my thinking in creating a painting. Carefully picked colors uncontrollably muddied by pooling water, a painting drained of color, an image re-composed by the arbitrariness of water, or even mildew attaching itself so persistently to paper in the humidity of the tropics, all become occasions to practice acceptance and inventiveness, to counteract self-doubt; reminders to stop postponing the moment, to be grounded in the simple joy and magic of the present; or just watch worries melt away when uncertain waters finally recede, exposing the discolored trace of unexpected possibilities.

When the traditional rainy season became hurricane season to us due to the frequency of storms, I learned a major lesson on change. As we both became even more perishable, I shared paper's vulnerability against the forces of nature, adapting to shared conditions in a shared environment and, once again, found myself instructed and empowered by this unassuming implement.

Many fellow watercolorists in St. Croix considered switching to canvas, then, for permanency and a higher price range. But my art and life were intimately braided together, so inextricably bound with paper as a confidant--not a liability. And since I was practicing living while creating art on paper, I considered myself rather fortunate to be alive and able to create one by means of the other.

I am grateful to all the miracle workers, the aggregate forces of minor agents that go into the tapestry of a work of art; the invariable integrity of these simple tools causes me to be constantly aware of my will as I work, not by repressing it, but simply letting it come and go.

I learned to resist the compulsion to rearrange phenomena unilaterally in accordance to my preferences, and to cultivate the formulation of deeper intentions in artistic endeavors. It becomes possible to calmly let design flow outward with the stimulating movement of water leaking off the page, spilling over into my life.

I came to paper out of necessity, with a mental dead end. I came away committed to the pursuit of aesthetic truth. Having to bend my ambitions to my means compelled me into accepting my own nature, as revealed on a soaked page.

When I fell in love with paper, I internalized its wisdom and it taught me, in turn, to become a medium.

--Maud Pierre-Charles

Adventure in Trinidad

A neighboring tenant in my Portsmouth, NH office building liked my ideas about raising start-up capital for treating new small businesses; with my help he began incorporating them into his *modus operandi* in instances where companies lacked other resources. It constituted a delicate process that required skill and stewardship.

Phil Taylor was consultant and coach to embryonic companies and tired, declining firms that were losing their way. He was skilled and provided necessary energy and insight to get things going. During the course of helping him with a few of his cases, I brought St Croix into the discussion, since it was much on my mind following my initial introduction to the island on a 1968 cruise. Subsequent vacation visits confirmed my attraction and I was convinced that I had located the place for me. I recalled the startling clarity of the sea and the pure white-crested waves breaking on the reef. Coconut palms leaned into the trades giving traction to their green-frond wheels. One warm day in the summer of 1970 Phil and I boarded an Eastern Airline flight to check out business opportunities on St Croix.

Investment in limited partnership shares by friends and family provided initial capital for exploring opportunities and finally commencing an investment firm in Christiansted, St Croix called Caribbean Capital, Ltd. One aspect of our financial services menu, as it developed, comprised small-business investment banking, modeled after Phil's Portsmouth effort. St Croix's small business community thirsted for funding, coaching and structuring, particularly during the growth years of the early '70s. In that capacity, a Trinidadian friend named Roy implored me to travel to that large, exotic island to help envision and fund a farm project that would allow him to return home to grow produce for market. Business was desultory during those hot summer days and I was able to delegate office management duties, so we set out for Trinidad and what became the most bizarre, interesting, and high-risk adventure of my life.

Roy had a policeman friend in the Marabella district of San Fernando, a major city on the north coast, who met us at the airport and became my host, he and his lady friend Rita, for the duration of the visit. Her relationship to the policeman looked, on the surface, as though they were mates, a perception that was soon contradicted. They were both hospitable and really made an effort to entertain me and make me comfortable. Roy joined us days, when the policeman was available, to tour the countryside in the man's Morris Minor, checking out available farm property.

We learned about a good piece of farmland for sale in the interior, equidistant from San Fernando and Princesstown, in a community called Eccles Village. We visited the property located in that attractive, tropical hinterland and viewed the verdant farm acreage from the road, what we could see of it. A hundred-acre section was for sale with the Princesstown Road running through. The lower, larger portion contained a wonderful display of citrus and coconut trees, both heavy with fruit. Apparently, out of respect for the owner, thieves did not remove the fruit. Teak and mahogany punctuated the rolling landscape. A stream ran through the property, promoting large stands of bamboo that gave accent to an Asian feeling. Above the road, on higher ground, stood a cocoa shed that hinted at possible rich, chocolate soil in which to cultivate cocoa. Valencia orange trees surrounded the shed. To this untrained eye the parcel looked good, very good! We got the name of the owner, a Chinese mercantile businessman in the capital, Port of Spain.

Permission was obtained by phone to go on the property. Roy was ecstatic at first blush. I learned, however, while talking with a few neighboring farmers, that the market for the grapefruit, which dominated the land along the road in neat, mature, multiple rows, was very limited. The Trinidad palette did not respond to grapefruit meat (sections) but did to the juice; that explained the plethora of ripe fruit hanging, unpicked, in the extended orchard. I learned later that boa constrictors did enjoy the tasty fruit and would gorge themselves, fall asleep in the trees and, at times, crash to the ground when supporting branches bent and broke. I once eased my Mazda over a boa stretched, asleep, across the sun-heated road, without disturbing it. Another anecdote concerning the rapacious reptiles came from a story in the Trinidad Guardian Sunday Supplement.

It was written that, over a period of time, a farmer's best producing Holstein milk cow had gone dry. Early morning milking produced drops where there had been gallons. In desperation he recruited the help of another farmer and they staked out the cowshed to determine if someone was stealing the milk. No one entered the shed during the night, yet the udder was barren when the a.m. milking was undertaken. They continued to guard the animal at night and were finally rewarded with the sight of a young boa contentedly suckling the milk. It had been that rascal, with perhaps help from some friends, who was drinking the cow dry.

Two thousand or more seedless, pink and white Marsh Grapefruit trees were ripe with large, sweet, juicy fruit that bent the lower tree-branches with their weight. That crop was what the land was best suited to grow on the lower section. The higher ground supported Valencia Oranges with fair success, a more popular fruit locally. Cocoa and coffee turned out to be insignificant, with only modest potential due to soil deficiencies. I received that important information by consulting with the University of the West Indies Agriculture Department. They sent a team out to actually see the land and test the soil. This contributed important perspective. They also made me aware of the newly chartered Agriculture Development

Bank, recently available to assist farmers, giving a new and positive element to our planning. They indicated that Roy might be eligible to borrow at low rates to develop the project, once we had completed the purchase of the property. That was positive sounding, but Roy would be the borrower, not me. I do not know how he really internalized the prospect. He would, at that point, be really committed to get to work and farm the land, and not just talk about it. It now strikes me that, in retrospect, he might have been getting cold feet, concerned that he was getting in over his head. It didn't occur to me then, so I didn't ask. Roy had originally talked about a "small farm." I assumed that he was on board for the larger version, a misguided assumption perhaps but one that Roy had ample opportunity to set straight.

It was never stated by him that he had doubts. The government agriculture people talked about planting cash crops of pineapple and onion, both popular items in the domestic market. They could be grown on the upper tract, along with intensified cultivation of the orange trees. Roy had voiced confidence that he could cultivate these and other garden produce. He appeared to be gung ho, and, consequently, so was I.

My jet plane took off for New England as I drew up plans for a limited-partnership syndication with which to finance the start-up of Roy's dream farm, and mine as well. I was able to raise $60,000 to be used to make a modest deposit on the land and provide funds to defray daily expenses while

Roy prepared to plant his gardens and get into production.

Roy took up residence in the cocoa shed and I rented a small farmhouse across the road from a lush section of the farm planted in robust grapefruit. I would open one to eat and the sweet juice would course down my arm until I could stop it with my mouth. The policeman and Rita moved in with me, she to cook, and he to impose security. The scene was tranquil; life had promise.

On Princesstown road, across from my rented house, on land surrounded by the farm property, stood a similar house owned by an East Indian farmer who maintained his property well, using the bottom level, under the elevated house, to store equipment, farm supplies, his cane wagon, and fodder for his animals. He was about my age, was rugged, and possessed a handsome water buffalo, a symbol of success among small farmers. He cared for the beast as one would a Mercedes Benz. The two were partners, both benefiting from their sugarcane-cultivating effort on a five-acre plot a mile down the road toward San Fernando. Beast and farmer worked hard and spent evening hours grooming and eating. Their annual journey to the distant sugar factory, with their wagonloads of ripe cane, was an event to celebrate. They delivered the best quality cane that the factory buyers weighed on their scales, and subsequently purchased, each harvest season. The synergy between farmer and beast was palpable. I wondered if Roy had that kind of enthusiasm and energy hidden below his phlegmatic exterior; ideally he did.

The interior of Trinidad resembles Southeast Asia culturally and demographically. East Indians, for the most part, work in the cane fields, cutting cane during harvest and cultivating during growing season. Water buffalo are preferred over tractors since the subsoil is largely clay and becomes glue-like when the rains descend. Houses are constructed of wood siding and roofing on wood-planked platforms supported by teak or purple heart posts, preferred for their insect resistance, secured in concrete footings. Concrete is a luxury whereas a variety of woods are readily available at reduced cost. Prized hardwoods needed protection from thieves bold enough to invade one's land to cut down a mature teak for the purpose mentioned. It can be very debilitating; we experienced it on the Eccles Village property with trees we had inventoried for future construction.

Hindu prayer flags fluttered from tall bamboo poles erected in front of the platform houses. Mosques, identified by their onion domes and brightly colored tiles and paint, were partially hidden in the ragged, quasi rain-forested farming communities where a hidden perfusion of coffee, cocoa, mango, avocado, various ground provision, citrus and papaya grew. Sugar cane, the cash crop, was more visible, occupying larger, cleared tracts along roads and pathways, lush and orderly in its perennial imperative. Living fences consisted of crowded, straight-growing plum saplings, sometimes formalizing roadside boundaries, as was the case with some of the in-town boundaries of our proposed farm. I found the aggregate rural effect exotic and enticing. I was at one with this sense of the cycle of nature and security that was emanating from the fact of endless tropical growth.

The Chinese owner agreed to a $10,000 non-refundable deposit, with the $90,000 balance due and payable at the end of one year. I felt that we could get bank financing or, that failing, be able to make a deal with the owner to finance the balance — a fuzzy plan in any real business sense, but I felt certain we could swing it. My stateside investors were prepared to put in more when the property was secured. Everything depended on us controlling the property. I needed Roy to start recruiting Trinidad investors; we had twenty more available limited-partner slots open before we had to close the offering with the maximum of thirty-six, based on Federal regulation in the US where the partnership was domiciled, all of the investors so far being American. There was a rich mother-lode of Trinidadians living in the US Virgin Islands, as well as on the mainland, who loved their homeland and would be interested in a Trinidad farm project, especially one that was forward-looking. Roy needed to work with me to plan a tour for the purpose of holding seminars for groups of Trinidad expatriates in order to explain our concept.

I felt the land reform, that had become the

popular course when independence from the British occurred, produced an impractical anomaly. The British plantation system, that had worked successfully, was largely erased and fragmented into small, ten-acre parcels for the indigent to live on and cultivate. Seed, fertilizer, livestock, and equipment were allocated, and farming machinery was made available, on a diminishing basis as it rusted and fell into disrepair. The government's vision was for an agricultural paradise benefiting workers rather than plantation owners.

Almost immediately the land reform beneficiaries sold or ate their seed and livestock and disposed of surviving gardening material, bought taxis and moved into town. The tiny plots reverted back to an unsupervised pool and lay fallow until the present. One difficult problem with cultivating the plots came from the soil that had been planted in cane for the past two centuries and was seriously depleted. Sugar cane also left soil insects that the hardy cane could withstand, but not garden crops. They were attacked from below and withered without hesitation. The destructive insects had caused an attempted transition to cotton to fail prior to distribution of the ten-acre plots. The socialist reform ultimately failed.

I had concluded that small lots should be reassembled into large tracts that could support the expensive effort to rejuvenate the soil and the expense of equipment needed to cultivate extensive crops. Sugar cane was still the universal cash crop, but was receiving diminished returns as the Brits withdrew Commonwealth support that European sugar beet production had been undercutting. Coconut copra was also only marginally rewarding, mainly for the oil used in soaps and for cooking oil, but also for the end product, shredded, dried coconut meat, still a world-wide delicacy, albeit abundantly available. The University Ag School and the new Agriculture Development Bank were positioning to assist farmers to develop new cash crops to supplant the old. Land prices were low and, I believe credit was available. This looked like opportunity-time to me.

In Eccles Village we had a great crop of grapefruit hanging in abundance from 2,000 odd trees, ready to harvest, actually beyond ready. The appropriate course was to find a process for packaging or canning the juice; the domestic market called for juice. That was the ploy then, to juice the wonderfully sweet fruit for sale in the domestic market. Time was against us. We were too late for the current crop year and would have to wait at least another year to implement a plan.

Roy needed to organize an onion-bed and also look into pineapple production. We had visited a notable pineapple plantation together and Roy made sounds that seemed to say that he could emulate what they were doing. I was not seeing much of him, nor was he galvanizing into farming activity. His stated purpose was to farm. Now, however, nothing much was happening. The front money I had raised was dwindling as expenses had begun to get traction.

Rita and I, plus the policeman, when he was present, were eating well by availing ourselves of farm produce: ground provision such as yam, sweet potato, eddo, and dasheen, an abundance of banana, mango, avocado, and papaya, and, of course, our wonderful citrus. Meat and fish were all that we needed to purchase for the table. Large prawn were brought in from the Atlantic, off the mouth of the Amazon River, by the extensive, government-subsidized, fleet of trawlers. An abundance of fish came from local nets; Mayero alone produced a surfeit that usually satisfied national demand.

Roy had stopped joining us for meals. He was made conspicuous by his absence. In retrospect I should have questioned this possible boycotting. At the time I exercised tolerance on grounds that the man had a life of his own and I should not, therefore, take issue with his absence and silence; he had always been a loner, an alcoholic trait. It occurs to me now that he might have been drinking and that would really explain his behavior.

At the time I had implicit faith in his sobriety. I wondered about his family. He had told me once about an ex-wife and children. I had not pursued the subject in depth, due perhaps to my own guilt about my neglect of wives and children. One day I noticed him driving a taxi on the road from San Fernando. When I finally paid him a late evening visit at the cocoa shed, he conceded succinctly that he owned the rattletrap taxi and needed to operate it to keep in funds. This seemed valid, but why had he not talked to me about it? A more valuable use of his time, under the circumstances, would have been to concentrate on developing a garden and organizing the land for planting. Possibly he had mentioned a need for funds, and maybe I had brushed him off or otherwise granted him short shrift. I do not remember having done so, but I did lean on him at times to get him going with the farming. Had I displayed too much impatience? Perhaps I did.

Roy was the principal in this farming endeavor. The two of us had formed a personal partnership for the purpose of meeting the general partnership liability requirement of the overall limited partnership. In effect, if the limited partners had no liability for the actions of the business entity beyond the loss of their investment, the general partner then needed to have the financial clout to cover general liability based on a statutory requirement, a multiple often times, let's say, of the maximum investment parameter of the limited partnership when all thirty six participations were sold.

It was to be Roy's business, as general partner, beyond the agreed portion of equity that was allocated for the limited partners, a maximum total of half the overall. In my partnership agreement with Roy, my fees were stated as a portion of his general partner equity. Roy was to receive the lion's share of ownership, a minimum of half, less my fee, stated as a small portion of his equity allocation. It was an elegant arrangement and was clearly delineated in the limited partnership prospectus.

Roy had a copy of the prospectus and I had carefully gone through it with him several times.

In all likelihood Roy could not read with any comprehension; he had little schooling and was basically ignorant, but, like so many Trinidadians, he was street-smart, and this is what he traded on. Any need for legal or business concurrence was met with a wise, all-knowing sort of smile, and affirmative nod. His handshake had always been weak and fish-like, lacking conviction. This was Roy. After my original vetting of him and our friendly agreement to commence this Trinidad undertaking, and subsequently my effort to produce the original funding, "without any financial investment on Roy's part," then it was a matter of trust between us. We were operating on his home ground and, so far, I was really on the financial hook. I did indeed trust him, despite general reference to, "tricky Trinies." Now, possibly, he was surreptitiously vacating the relationship to pursue another course. In retrospect it certainly seems so. He had become untrustworthy — perhaps. This is conjecture; nevertheless informed.

Roy had, as a result of my badgering, brought in a single $5,000 investor, a nearby elderly farmer friend. I handed Roy the necessary paperwork with which to sign up the new limited partner, wrote a receipt, and, subsequently, deposited the money in our general account, home to our dwindling treasury. This experience had occurred early in the Eccles Village farm genesis. And I remember Roy, at the time, giving me an odd look as I received the money from him.

The elderly farmer-investor was looking on intently. I complimented them both and then, in an aside, urged Roy to bring in more investors. We had plenty of room for more under the 36-limited partner maximum imposed by Massachusetts where the business was registered and where all the investors, except the new man, who was a Trinidadian, were residents. Roy said that he thought he could find some additional investors, wrinkled his weathered brow and gave me the fleeting, all knowing smile. Once more, in hindsight, I recognize that the man did not understand his need to generate new investor funding if his (our) project was to get off the ground. I was there to assist in the investment effort, and raised the initial funding with which to perform the early exploratory work. The time had long since arrived when he needed to organize a corps of investors to float the enterprise until the farm could generate sufficient cash flow to conduct operations. I could put form to the financing and talk with potential investors; group investor seminars had been suggested at the outset. Now Roy had to follow up. He was the principal and needed to act that way. It was critical that he be in agreement on that fundamental issue. A wry smile was not enough assurance — as I have now been made aware.

I returned, one afternoon, to my house in Eccles Village, to find a small crowd of locals witnessing a loud verbal altercation. A male and a female voice alternated accusations and angry responses. I worked my way toward my house and was joined by Rita, the owner of the female voice. The male counter-voice belonged to the old farmer next door who raised chickens for sale. Gradually the hysteria was explained to me. Rita had approached the old man with an offer to barter two of his chickens for a screw. They had jumped into his bed and when finished he decided it was not worth two, but only one chicken. Rita, indignant over the breach of contract, had descended on the old man to right the wrong.

I was astounded by the barter arrangement and asked her why it had been necessary to obtain the chickens in that manner; why had she not asked me for the money? Her response was touching in a perverse way. She said that she had wanted to surprise me with a nice chicken dinner.

I searched for and found a freezing and packaging plant that could possibly convert our Eccles Village seedless grapefruit to fancy sections and package and flash-freeze them. It was located in the remote Point Cedros area of the island. The same place could juice the grapefruit and package the juice in cardboard containers. I had the possible answer to our dilemma of what to do with the grapefruit. The packaging and freezing operation was part of a modern, privately owned, shrimp processing factory. The owner thought the equipment good for the purpose that I proposed. He also owned several shrimp trawlers that fished the disputed waters off the mouth of the Amazon River, bringing home large prawns, inhabitants of those feeding grounds. Restaurants craved the creatures in order to create the culinary prize, butterflied, broiled, stuffed shrimp. The prawns were considered gold.

The shrimp company owner was an attractive, hard-working businessman. During our conversations he shared with me information about Peruvian backers who had just financed two new trawlers about to join his fleet. He introduced me to a few men who were visiting from Peru. They seemed cordial and were attentive toward me, listening to what I had to say, and inquiring about aspects of my business there in Trinidad. They explained that their international holding company was owned and backed by an impressive array of "Standard and Poor's 500" companies. They were dressed conservatively, out of keeping with that rural setting, and were impressively businesslike. I was attracted to that entire Point Cedros concept, including the Peruvian backers, and I saw possible potential for benefiting the Eccles Village enterprise.

Rita and the policeman moved on after a few months and my interest in Point Cedros made Eccles village seem less accessible because it was in the other direction from Marabella. The shrimp factory backers from Peru were showing an interest in financially backing our Eccles Village farm and discussion of money was on the table. It was becoming evident to me that the athletic looking, well dressed gentlemen from Peru were more than mere businessmen. They knew more about me than was possible from our brief exposure, unless they had access to my Marine Corps records or — the *dossier* prepared two decades earlier when I had departed active military duty and made inquiries at the CIA. The so-called Peruvians appeared to be organizing a clandestine operation and sought to use our businesses as cover for their political information gathering. I was on the brink of becoming a clandestine operative in Trinidad, my host country.

When I departed my residence in Eccles Village for a small apartment in Marabella, I talked with Roy and found him distant and uncommunicative. I told him what I had been doing without bringing the CIA into it. I had, at the outset, at Roy's request, smuggled a Mauser 7.5 mm pistol with ammo and a new 12-guage shotgun, also with ammo, into the country for him, for his protection and to guard the crops and hardwood trees from thieves. I had carried the Mauser in Korea as a concealed, extra weapon, to defend against infiltrators who had been an active threat. He was in charge of both.

We talked about the need to start grooming the fruit trees and to begin laying out the beds and fields for new crops. We discussed the timing for planting, management of water from the stream, and the need for piping and pumps for irrigation. Bamboo was proliferating along the stream, wasting water. It sorely needed thinning. Roy had done very little so far to prepare and maintain the place and the meter was running on our deposit. I explained that I would be at Point Cedros or Marabella working that end of things. We had to work separately, up to a point. We also needed more investment capital.

I had inadvertently kept an extra box of pistol ammo at the apartment in Marabella. An oversight; I should have given it to Roy. On my return one evening I realized someone had gone through my stuff and taken the ammo, leaving a few rounds scattered through my clothing to let me know that they knew.

The policeman had been very curious about me and about my activities and had really kept close tabs. He was in touch with a few senior police. Roy, too, had a close friend who was a senior police inspector. Roy introduced me, showing clear respect for the man, so I, too, held him in respectful regard. Now those powerful senior police were apprised of my indiscretion concerning the ammo and, assumedly, the weapon that went with it. I was aware that a mandatory four-year sentence would be levied against a person in possession of an unlicensed firearm. I was certainly now under observation.

The youngest daughter of the family upstairs at the house in Marabella, Jenny, was being groomed to become a prostitute in order to bring money into family coffers. She was the most attractive of three sisters. The oldest was married and had a good secretarial job in Port of Spain. The other was the scullery maid of the household, a veritable slave. In fact, she might not have been a sister at all, what with reports that you hear of slavery in the third world. The parents were clearly money oriented. Boboy, the father, had a responsible job at the Texaco refinery; they operated a small grocery under the front part of their house, and the oldest daughter brought money home every month. Now they expected Jenny to do her part. She was a blithe spirit, not at all accepting of her father's mandate that she become a whore. She asked if she could move in with me on the basis of a mock relationship, as a ploy to postpone her imposed new career.

I was game, but in the process became unpopular with her kid brother who resented my intrusion into family matters. It was he who had apparently searched my belongings, found the ammo, and reported to the policeman who subsequently instructed the lad to scatter a few rounds among my clothes. The brother was fifteen, Jenny was eighteen and I was forty-five.

Jenny was employed as an office worker following secretarial school and had been discharged without proper notice or termination pay for resisting the advances of the office manager. The Department of Labor heard her complaint and awarded her a sizeable severance, paid by the guilty firm. Boboy took the money and, among other things, bought the largest Holstein milk cow I have ever seen. Jenny insisted on being certified as half-owner of the cow. Smart! She had become a person of means despite her father having purloined the large award, $20,000 in BWI dollars, which had been legally awarded to Jenny. Nevertheless, she had influence in family circles because everyone knew that Boboy had taken the money that was hers. And she held title to half interest in the Holstein. The brother had a growing resentment. Now Jenny and I had partnered up which further exacerbated the lad's ill feelings. She did not want to be alone with her father or her brother. Boboy and wife Dolly were willing to let things slide for the time being. The brother did not like it. Jenny was supposed to be a whore and I concluded that he wanted to pimp for her. That was to be his presumed role and he did not care to relinquish the position of authority.

Jenny was grateful that I supported her and gave her shelter. I had assumed the role of boyfriend for her family's edification, in order to alleviate the need for her to hit the streets as a neophyte prostitute. If the relationship with the American worked out, it would suffice, so long as he was generous enough with their daughter that there was spillover for them as well. This was the plot that Jenny had skillfully set in motion. I was game. I took her out in my small Japanese car to teach her to drive. That was a move to advise her parents that my intentions were serious. My car had become Jenny's as well. Despite the intrigue, the driving lessons were hilarious.

My interest in Point Cedros brought me in

contact with the owner of St Anne's, a beautiful plantation in operation since its inception during British colonial rule. The owner, Macgregor, had switched from copra to cocoa and coffee early on, thanks to an abundance of chocolate soil necessary for cultivation of cocoa in particular. Mac had also been forward looking, switching emphasis from the old-fashioned, long-stemmed copra coconut trees to an African dwarf tree that stays close to the ground and produces large, yellow, so called "water nuts" because they contain an abundance of coconut water, along with a tasty jelly before it forms into the white meat. Those had become the cash crops: cocoa, coffee and water nuts, no longer the labor-intensive copra that had drastically diminished in net value. Mac retained thousands of long-stemmed trees to which he leased picking rights so others could make the copra effort for small returns. Again, advanced in his methods, Mac planted lime trees interspersed among the tall coconut, as a second crop. The limes had flourished and were also jobbed out for others to cultivate and harvest. The fruit was large, sweet, and deep green in color, unlike the yellowish key lime that is small and tart. Finally, to his great credit, he was experimenting with beef cattle to graze in the great dappled expanses of his copra groves, beneath the stork-like coconut palms, to hopefully develop into a third crop, where there had been only the copra.

Trucks arrived on Wednesdays and Thursdays to load up with water nuts for the weekend crowd at Queen's Park Savannah in the capitol, Port of Spain. The nuts would be iced in tubs fabricated from dissected oil drums mounted on car axles and wheels. The purveyor of the nuts would swiftly decapitate the iced nut, allowing a small opening to drink from, a full quart of refreshing water. Coconut water consumed, the customer would return the nut to the purveyor to have it surgically split in half and returned with a chip cut from the husk to serve as a spoon for the jelly *entree*. The effortless cutting of the tough husk was performed with the point-weighted blade of a cutlass, designed to cut sugar cane. Most Trinidadian men have a comfortable attachment to their cutlass, as though it is an appendage. The water nut guys loved to demonstrate their inherent skills. The performance was important to the enjoyment of gurgling the cold liquid, and consuming the fresh, semi-sweet jelly.

Cocoa was the mainstay and I was able to watch as great trays of beans, on flat drawers, were extended out from the sheds on sunny days. At intervals a barefoot worker would rhythmically move between the rows, deftly turning the beans over with his big toes to dry evenly. He was referred to as a "dancer." Coffee was dried on trays as well, but without the ceremonial dancing. Coffee beans were turned over using wood rakes. Also a staple, it does not, however, bring the premium price of cocoa, which requires the special chocolate soil. Soil requirements for coffee are not as restrictive; consequently, more is grown and profit margins are smaller.

St Anne's Plantation was a model for tropical farms. Macgregor had established a tradition of good maintenance and farm management that was well conceived and skillfully executed. A small sandstone quarry supplied crushed stone to layer on the roads and pathways as a check against mud-producing rains. He referred to this as "stoning the roads." After his wife died, Mac yearned to return to Scotland and family there. He was looking for a new owner who would carry on his proven management practices. This was, of course, a blue ribbon farm and would yield immediate returns if one wanted a 24-7 job in farming. I was tempted and held long discussions with the man. He was lonely and enjoyed my company, and I his. The implication was that he would stay on as long as needed and would possibly retain a piece of the business and even finance the balance. He was that anxious to have the right man in place, allowing him some latitude for travel. On his own initiative, Mac started to clear a home site for me on a bluff looking across the Serpent's Mouth to Venezuela. He was far ahead of me and my ability to make such a commitment. It was most appealing but would, once again, shackle me, restricting what I saw as my freedom. Anyway, other events intervened to disallow further plans for a purchase or partnering with Mac.

My emerging theory for farming in Trinidad was to emulate the British colonial model by trading with other islands via small freighters, some freezer ships, some reefer and others designed for dry cargo, establishing a bartering methodology whereby islands concentrate on their most successful crops and barter for crops they cannot raise effectively, but that other islands specialize in and are particularly adept at growing. This inter-island technique falls under the category known as the "Principle of Relative advantage," and had been discussed in classes at Georgetown School of Foreign Service. The flash freezing and packaging operation at Point Cedros would enable shipping to the far reaches of the Caribbean and northern South America. I had heard that a small, reefer freighter belonging to a gentleman living on St Croix, who had extensive agricultural holdings on St Lucia, might be for sale. I attempted to initiate talks with the man once when I stopped over on business with my old investment firm, but he was not available. He owned the hotel where I spent a Sunday afternoon lounging by the giant salt-water pool. I was also told that he was father to a beautiful daughter.

Key to commencing this great experiment was funding. The Peruvian group was showing interest in supporting my Trinidad activities contingent on an agreement to help advance their interests in that country. They were keen to be apprised of attitudes and activities of that socialist government headed by Eric Williams, an avowed communist sympathizer. This was during Fidel Castro's triumphant revolutionary period when his trusted lieutenant, Che Guevara was also exporting the revolution to mainland South America and was becoming a cult figure in the process. It did not surprise me that the CIA was busy in the Caribbean.

Clearly there was something going on in Eric William's left-leaning government that was not being publicized. Too many police were moving around without assigned jurisdictions, operating in small groups or squads. The infamous Inspector Boroughs headed up one such group known as the "flying squad," (V S Naipaul referred to this type of activity in GUERRILLAS.) I had met Boroughs at the policeman's house in Marabella, where he would make surprise visits while I was present, lounge around, have a drink and a plate of food and even, at times, lie on the floor to take a nap. He was curious about me in a veiled way and, I suppose, wanted assurance that I was not doing what I was now undertaking to do, spying. It was said that the Inspector was a very rough customer and answered only to the head of government. I did not, at that time view him as a threat.

Another high-level policeman was an acquaintance of Roy who introduced him to me as "my close friend." This close tie was reinforced over a few subsequent unscheduled meetings. Name forgotten, he was an established friend of Roy, so I also considered him my friend by association. He appeared supportive of our business aspirations and was helpful in opening doors for me at Departments of Agriculture and Immigration. I now see that he too was interested in my presence in Trinidad. The red flag was certainly raised when ammunition was discovered in my Marabella apartment. The entire Police Department was alerted before I even met the men from Peru, I now must assume.

My final dealings with the Marabella policeman involved Rita. I accidentally observed an incident in the house she was sharing with him. I was climbing the stairs unannounced and heard loud voices and Rita's cries of pain. I rushed up the steps in time to see the policeman straddling her on the floor and slapping her face hard with alternating sweeping blows, striking her unmercifully. She was stifling her screams as best she could, as if to admit guilt of sorts, as though she deserved the harsh treatment. When he became aware of my presence he ceased, casually stood and welcomed me as though nothing had transpired. Rita scuttled away like a wing-broken bird and left the house. I had the idea that I was somehow a part of that violent encounter, that Rita was being punished for her behavior, or lack of it, toward me, and the breach was significant enough to enrage him.

Now I believe that, when Rita and I closed the Eccles Village residence and drifted apart, the policeman was deprived of his ability to closely monitor me. I wonder if she had developed feelings for me and did not, therefore, wish to continue spying for him. Perhaps she refused to play that role any longer. Anyway, I resented his maltreatment of the woman who had been kind to me. The policeman had an ugly side that I could not ignore. I subsequently found an opportunity to repay him for brutalizing Rita. It was a rehearsed blow to his solar plexis, high up beneath his heart, just below his rib cage, that caught him right and left him writhing in pain and trying to catch his breath. He was a rugged man, so a single blow had to be disabling. I left the place and heard later that he had been hospitalized. If so, it must have been for dramatic effect. Rita, the policeman and I were no longer in that strange, tripartite relationship.

I had little concern over police observation of me until the incident in which Jenny's brother illicitly discovered the ammunition in my Marabella apartment. At first I assigned it to boyish revenge for my role in protecting his sister. Only later did I reason that the policeman had become privy to the damning information, and may have even put the lad up to it in the first place. I was simultaneously in discussions with the men from Peru and had agreed to commence my clandestine career, a move that had red lights going off behind my eyes, but also possessed financial allure. I was *ex officio* a Marine Corps Captain and therefore ready for danger. I was blinded, however, to the awareness the police possessed concerning my potential for mischief. I felt this spying mission amounted to little more than harmless reporting, nothing criminal.

I had been introduced to my Trinidad contact, a man who managed a part government-owned manufacturing operation. He asked me to visit his office to establish the parameters of our relationship. I complied and we talked in general terms, set a date for my return and I left to wend my innocent way back to Marabella, oblivious of having crossed the line and become a "guerrilla."

I had business with the elusive Roy to inform him of my grand scheme for juicing grapefruit for market, and packaging and freezing grapefruit sections along with other fruit such as pineapple. I also wanted to apprise him of Estate St Anne and its potential. Roy was not there in Eccles Village, nor was there evidence of work having been accomplished on the land. I was told that he still lived in the shed, but was away most of the time. Not good!

My scheduled return to the manufacturer was met with frightened, saucer-eyed looks from the office staff as I was handcuffed by Boroughs to be transported to police headquarters in San Fernando. No hint was given as to the charge, but I knew my career as a spy was being nipped in the bud before I was able to do any spying. I had been detected in this role before the opportunity to spy was offered to me. I compromised the men from Peru from the moment they took me on. The policeman in Marabella had me dead to rights before I agreed to sell my soul to finance the Eccles Village farm. Remembering the old silent films featuring the Keystone Cops, I could have been one of them with my fumbling effort. Or, more recently, Jimmy Breslin's book, THE GANG THAT COULDN'T SHOOT STRAIGHT offered role models for me to follow, and I did.

The police had me write a complete description of my activities in Trinidad. They informed me that charges were being brought by Roy's farmer friend who had invested $5,000 in the farm project, for embezzling his money. Roy apparently served as witness to my crime and was supporting the case against me. That is what I wrote about in my statement, my side of the so-called embezzlement. I also alluded to my connection with the industrial manager as a new friendship and a budding business association. I knew very little about the man. The police revealed to me that he had been killed by the "Flying Squad" while he tried to escape, a warning in case I was considering running from my so-called "embezzlement" charge. My spy contact was dead and I was being held on a charge of embezzlement. It did not add up, unless the obfuscation could be attributed to the American embassy, which must have become involved by now and had possibly concocted this script as a face-saving concession to ameliorate the real problem.

I believed the police were building their case against me concerning matters of national security. Roy must have been complicit and had obviously, long since, vacated our relationship. In his bewilderment, he had likely disclosed what he perceived to be our financial plan for acquiring and operating Eccles Village farm. The American Embassy, in damage control mode, was offering the "embezzlement" cover-up. I was being shown in the light of Yankee opportunism. I do not now believe anyone in Trinidad knew what was meant by a limited partnership.

Surprisingly I was released by the police. However, they did keep my passport, admonishing me to remain nearby and available to them. They must have felt that this was a large spy operation and they might catch others falling into the net by using me as bait. No one approached to take the bait. I removed myself from the Eccles Village project, relinquishing the deposit. The farm was not going to take off and fly at this point. Roy had disappeared and I could not proceed alone. I parked my car and looked over the land from the Princesstown Road and wished it were ours to farm along the lines I had developed. The Chinese owner continued in his role of community leader and would set a table and two chairs under a large mango tree Saturday mornings so villagers could consult with him about crops and land leasing arrangements, pay their rent, borrow for the purchase of a water buffalo, ask advice about a sick child, etc. This was a timeless tradition and I respected the man for the role he played. I was gone — out of there.

I had a dream of living out my years in Trinidad as a farmer, revolutionizing the marketing of fruit crops by utilizing flash-freezing and packaging techniques and transporting our crops inter-island to barter for needed products not produced at home. I am fundamentally attracted to the society of farming people and commercial fishermen. I wanted to, and did to an extent, engage my brush with acrylic paint to record the culture of platform houses and Hindu prayer flags fluttering, and the partnership between water buffalo and their masters. My dream was unraveling and the new reality was Inspector Boroughs and the Flying Squad.

I gravitated to the capital city, Port of Spain, where I became an active supporter of the Alcoholic Clinic and Rehabilitation Center housed in St Ann's Asylum overlooking Queen's Park Savannah in a Charles Adams-like group of Gothic buildings. It was there that the "cure" was administered to hapless alcoholics who had arrived by one means or another. The process was well organized, and the administrator was a qualified, fortyish Brit. The process allowed the drunk to continue imbibing his rum while also ingesting doses of a chemical compound designed to react to alcohol by making the patient ill. Dosage was gradually increased until the problem drinker was confronted with need to cease the alcohol or expire, or so it seemed. This induced illness would be continued until the drinker decided that alcohol was just not worth the suffering. At that auspicious moment the twelve-step program for alcoholics would be introduced as a rational alternative. The drunk was allowed to clean up and attend a meeting to commence his education into alcoholic reform. A series of meetings were held over a period of weeks while the patient convalesced. The patient's family was invited in to share in the rehabilitation process; testimonials were emotionally delivered and the day arrived when each patient graduated and returned to the larger community. This constituted the "cure" for alcoholics in Trinidad.

I often found myself sitting in empty churches meditating and even praying, an activity quite unfamiliar to me, asking for extended guidance and protection. I was following instinct, ephemerally aware that my Higher Power had allowed me to survive thus far. The police were momentarily poised to scoop me and I was fearful about the next step after that. I was praying in the foxhole mode whereby I promised Him that I would reform my ways if he got me through this crisis. It was working and I had the continuing need to stay as close as possible to God; thus the empty churches, on weekdays, where I could commune, unattended and unobserved. I was calm, almost serene, a term I always scoffed at as being weak and mushy.

I was about to be confronted with charges and a Magistrate who would understand little about me and my underlying issues and who would adjudicate my fate. I anticipated a mock trial. Nevertheless, I wanted to set the record straight on the embezzlement charge. It would require an educational effort in court and I was preparing mentally to conduct class. As I was sitting in empty pews, I had a sense of peace, that things would work out. I was having a spiritual experience. God was embracing this foolish, recovering drunk.

Once again I was in the police station in San Fernando, being treated roughly, with no recourse to rational questioning. I was being formally accused and brought up on a charge of embezzling funds from our farming project. There were no charges mentioned concerning the possession of illegal arms and ammunition or espionage, for which my contact person, the industrialist, was shot and killed. Reference to Inspector Boroughs and his death squad was not invoked, just the exaggerated reference to my receipt of the $5,000 investment that was interpreted as embezzlement. That was really a stretch, particularly inasmuch as the funds were deposited in the general checking account of the farm project, and remained there to the best of my knowledge. Anyway, I guess the obfuscation served a face-saving purpose for the Trinidad Court and our embassy.

I was transported to the "Royal Gaol" in Port of Spain and deposited in a medieval dungeon occupied by fourteen or fifteen other prisoners. High stonewalls had one or two miniscule barred windows at the top allowing scant light. A large, iron, cross-strapped door had a small observation window and a small iron sliding door near the bottom for the purpose of depositing containers of food and water on the dungeon floor twice daily. No eating utensils were offered so we made do with our hands and shared the large water container. The stone floor had a hewn canal at the far end of the room, with a trickle of water for sanitary purposes. Two heavy six by ten foot wood benches were in the center for prisoners to lie on in continual relays around the clock. The perennial darkness erased any demarcation between day and night after a short time in residence. The thirty-foot cell dimensions were asymmetric, arranged haphazardly around the older, inner structure.

Cockroaches abounded, particularly behind and between the iron strappings of the door. They were albino due to the lack of sunlight, hundreds of white cockroaches. National Geographic Magazine should have been notified.

After a few days in the receiving dungeon, I was placed in a smaller cell with another man who had a lighter complexion than other prisoners. He must have been part Hispanic. We each had a bench to lie on, a vast improvement. He said nothing to me and I responded in kind, reasoning that this coupling was contrived to get information from me, so why bother to talk. We were not allowed a phone call to arrange for a lawyer, but I had no one to call anyway. I needed to keep my cool and allow things to play out. I am an American citizen and I felt it stood for something. They would not hang me I reckoned, at least not immediately. After a week of lounging in the Royal Gaol, I was transported to the main prison in the hinterlands and placed in a cell with ten or eleven Afro-Trinidadians.

The new accommodations were smaller, more intimate and four centuries newer. We were thrust together more tightly, but the air circulation was much improved. We were allowed exercise periods in which to move around in a walled yard similar to runs designed for zoo animals. The rice and beans, with parsimonious slivers of meat or fish, and the occasional glint of a green vegetable, bode well for survival, and was in stark contrast with meals served in the white cockroach lounge of the Royal Gaol. I did not feel as though any of my new cellmates were necessarily watching me, but I did feel ostracized and distrusted. They were a sullen bunch and gave me little notice. I perceived that one man was the leader, a person others deferred to. He had murdered his wife and had no regrets. He was articulate and positive in his outlook. I listened to his dialogue with the others and gradually interjected observations and anecdotes that complemented what he was saying. He was my hope for protection if any of the others became annoyed with me. I began to understand that prison leadership accrued to those who had committed capital crimes, murder in most cases. The more heinous the murder, the higher the position in the prison hierarchy the inmate attained. Top leadership, at the time, was assigned to the serial killer of British tourist ladies whom the murderer entertained, wined and dined, and then systematically dispatched, burying them in his garden. This leadership figure had been scheduled to hang, but enjoyed a number of postponements for a variety of legal reasons. He held sway. Inmates and security guards alike deferred to him, a man who had killed twenty or so of England's fairest. When his garden could accommodate no more, he commenced to bury victims on others' property. That was his undoing. Had his garden been larger, his freedom, as well as his life, would have extended longer.

This was the time of "black militancy" in the States, and elsewhere as well, since the world wanted to emulate the USA. The supreme leader in the Trinidad Prison was also the supreme black militant. As such, he set an example for the others. I believe I was the only Caucasian in the institution of, perhaps, four thousand. The odds for me were not good, especially after the top dog received news of my incarceration. He would rant about the inclusion of white destroying the purity of the prison population. My guy, a lesser murderer, took care of me. He cautioned me to stay close, and I did. In years following, when I have related this story, I've been suspected of sexual capitulation as payment for him protecting my white ass. Certainly, in the American penal system, that would have been a fair assumption. There had been no thought of it on my part, and no hint that I had an obligation on my protector's part. If the obligation had existed, I wonder which way it would have gone. I cannot imagine that I would have conducted myself differently. Snicker away, if you must.

Despite having murdered his wife, my guy was not serving a long sentence, four or five years at most in prison. The court was lenient due to the extenuating circumstances influencing his crime. He had an outside wife, a woman younger than his actual wife, and a family with her that he was engaged with, having no children otherwise. The regular wife had a growing resentment concerning the arrangement. When he returned from being away a few days, tired from his activity with the other family, and went to bed, she silently entered the darkened bedroom with a razor blade and cut his two wrists, tendons and all. The man awoke, feeling the sting of the razor, realized he was seriously injured, arose from the bed, and headed down the stairs to find transportation to the hospital, blood-soaked sheets wrapped around his wrists. Anticipating this move, his wife removed a kettle of boiling water from the stove and poured it over his bare departing back, shoulders and head. He literally crawled to a neighbor who drove him to the hospital, nearly bled out. There he was treated, given blood, sewn up, tendons were imperfectly reattached and his burn rehabilitation was started. For two years he convalesced and, by dint of physical therapy and plastic surgery, was finally well enough to remove a turned leg from his kitchen table, pay his wife a visit, and beat her to death. He then walked to the police station, at some distance, and turned himself in.

The action my protector took represented the unrelenting principle of "an eye for an eye." Society forgave his crime due to circumstances and, most importantly, the court exercised leniency in sentencing the man. He was seen as justified in his action, a person of character. I was his ward for the duration. He needed an audience to hear his story, one that would respond sympathetically. I performed that role. I listened and gave informed responses to his need for understanding and respect. That was my role in the partnership and, by performing it, I established parity in return for his protection.

I heard nothing from the American Embassy. I did not really expect them to be forthcoming. A Red Cross representative did inquire in order to be assured that I was being treated OK, which I was. Jenny, her sister and brother-in-law visited to cheer me up and relate that I might be released on bail. They were excited. This was unexpected news and was, of course, very pleasing to me, even though it was not *a fait accompli*. The young people were apparently behind it. A few days later, much to my amazement, I was released, and they picked me up in my car, now Jenny's, for the journey back to the Belmont suburb of Port of Spain, to take up residence with Jenny's sister, Joan, and husband Leroy, sharing their two bedroom apartment.

Finally I could phone the States to talk with my mother and attempt to explain my plight and get the wheels turning to raise money for my legal defense against the spurious charge of embezzlement. In the course of my convoluted explanation I learned that my dad had died while I languished in prison. Sidney had slipped away without waiting for me. I did not know what to say, or who to say it to.

Naturally, all bets were off concerning Eccles Village farm and St Anne's Plantation at Point Cedros. The elderly farmer was returned his $5,000. I wondered about the true origin of that disputed money. The single, brief time I met the old-timer I wondered fleetingly where he had located that much disposable cash. I reflected later, after the fact, that the police, in a sort of sting operation, might have set me up. My legal team was contracted and we inched toward a trial date in the undefined future.

I asked Jenny how they had arranged my bail. I had heard that a bail bond could be issued only against real estate collateral with a verifiable value of 150% of the bail amount mandated by the court. My bail was set at $20,000 BWI so $30,000 of real estate would have to be pledged. How had these young people managed the collateral?

There was little chance that I would leave the island since the police had my passport, so an arrangement was made for payment of a fee to the bailer, calculated with good assurance that I would show up in court for the trial date. Jenny had gone to her father to sell her half of the Holstein cow to him. Whatever leverage she used with him worked, he paid her cash and she delivered it to the bailer. Then Jenny and her sister and brother-in-law signed a note to pay the bailer in the event that I jumped ship. In effect, I had really been bailed out by Jenny's share of the Holstein cow, that and what leverage she had with her father to convert her ownership to cash. She was expressing her gratitude for my support when she was being forced into a career she didn't want. I had blocked her father and brother who both saw whoring as her best career calling.

Art filled my days along with my active support of the alcohol addiction program at St Ann's Asylum that focused my spiritual awareness, reminding me that faith had carried the day during recent tough times. I needed to understand this and embrace it. God was clearly my protector; my young friends were conduits of God's grace.

We attended movies many evenings, together, as a cohesive, happy unit, Jenny, her older sister Joan, Joan's husband Leroy, and me, the middle-aged honky. Horror movies were the fare in both the ornate old theaters on the periphery of Queen's Park Savannah. The films were mostly British, with wonderful acting and direction. They were world-class horror films, two at a showing, double features. The theaters also offered beverage and snack bars dispensing full-course dinners and special delights such as roti. I could happily live on roti alone. It consists of a pizza pie-size, round, wheat flour tortilla-type bread fried on a flat, cast iron grill and filled with curried delights that were folded into the roti: beef, shrimp, chicken, or potato, each a treat. A book would be needed to describe the myriad ways to prepare this gastronomical art form. Every Trinidad woman has her own unique style for preparing the genre. Suffice it to say, the food complemented any movie.

The theaters were commodious, allowing ample room for the multitude of youth that added theatrical flavor. This was a forum for social interaction. The young people were part of the production, posturing in carnival garb which the men continued to display year 'round for comic affect: exaggerated hats, brightly colored shirts, clown-like neckties, and such. The young women appeared in their coolest threads, vying for fashion queen honors. Movies did not start 'til 10 pm, so a double feature with a thirty-minute intermission, ran ᶜtil 2am. We would return to the apartment sated by the experience.

Carnival season commenced and we joined the crowds in Port of Spain for the "tramp" during *Jou 'vert*. We followed the steel band from the suburb of Belmont through the streets and danced to the competing force of hundreds of steel pans when bands came together at intersections attempting to play each other down. Eardrums strained and knees buckled from the long day's exertion; we had started before dawn that first day. Queen's Park Savannah, with the race track and cricket fields, provided the nexus for the final steel band competition in which regional winners gathered, arranged on iron-pipe-constructed, truck-drawn, multi-wheeled platforms that flexed and vibrated rhythmically to the music. A chaotic symphony of steel pans rose through the sinuous, exaggerated limbs of the great samán trees; lions in the zoo listened in silence, unable to compete.

Now the streets were challenged to contain the brass bands arranged on cane trucks blaring their amplified contributions to the bedlam. Close behind followed troops performing choreographs and displaying flesh, partially concealed by costumes created in the intervening year since the previous carnival. The Prince and Princess floats joined the procession to be judged in the Savannah, followed by the extravagant King and Queen floats. Now was the *denouement*, when winners of these national competitions were announced. Regional calypso winners had arrived, with their tents strategically positioned, to fill the night with music and humor, delivered in the spirit of ancient balladeers, as they too vied for national honors.

Everywhere there was rum and beer but few got drunk. Exertion offset the debilitating effects of alcohol. Energy and excitement nullified drunkenness, at least for awhile. Later, when activity slowed and exhaustion descended, inebriation asserted itself. I had never felt so much crowd .energy nor witnessed such abandon. This had been the excising required to release negative feelings and memories. I was being bid farewell by a country I had fallen in love with and then attempted to betray.

A year expired before I had my day in court, two days actually. The Magistrate dismissed the feeble defense my legal team offered with a dismissive wave of hand, as though brushing off a fly. He then entered into a tirade aimed at foreigners who came to Trinidad to cheat the disadvantaged populace. He shouted a general warning to outsiders to stay away, and that Americans in particular were not welcomed. He found me guilty as accused, never giving me a chance to explain about our Eccles Village farm project and the financial vehicle fashioned to fund it.

Then, to my amazement, the Judge granted me a suspended sentence, returned my passport and announced that I was free to go. The case was closed. It had consisted entirely of empty legal rhetoric. Defense and prosecution had gone back and forth nitpicking about the meaning of the term embezzlement. My side claimed that I could not possibly embezzle from my own company, displaying an abysmal ignorance about business matters; the prosecutor claimed that it was not my company, indicating a bit more business acumen. The prosecutor was correct but, in a sense, I was contractually a minority owner. Roy was the principal, and it was he who had requested my help and voluntarily entered into the Limited Partnership Agreement with the others — and me. These facts needed to be spoken for the record, but never were. Our rights, as a legal entity, were being abrogated. We actually constituted the injured parties in the proceeding. Oh well, they had their funny little mock trial, for which I was a veritable prisoner on Trinidad for close to two years, albeit wonderful years.

The usual requirement for a tax clearance letter was waived. I said goodbye to Jenny and the others, promising to stay in touch. Monies had been repaid to all parties. I traveled to the airport and boarded a jet plane, trundled to the end of the runway, and — paused. I gripped the arms of my seat, expecting the police to board the plane, seize me and transport me back to the slammer to await the consequences of espionage and gun charges. The ship moved forward gathering speed, left the ground, climbed, banked, and faced north to begin our flight to America. I was returning to where it all began for me.

-- Preston Doane

ABOUT THE AUTHORS

Don Cox and his wife first tasted St. Croix in 2004, liked what they found, and moved here permanently in 2009. A retired teacher of physics and student of the Milky Way, he kills tan-tan, fixes stuff, SCUBA dives, and writes stories, most of them meant to urge young people of all ages to add mathematical approaches to their tools for understanding the world.

Preston Doane:

ADVENTURE IN TRINIDAD recounts an early episode in my four-decade Caribbean experience. I continue today as an artist living on St. Croix, at safe anchor inside the reef.

Patricia Gill, a retired academic and long-time resident of St. Croix, is the author of "Buddhoe", "The Cape of the Arrows", "The Americans Came", and "America's Paradise: 1936", novels based on the history of St. Croix. Her poetry has been published in The Caribbean Writer and the Hampton - Sidney Poetry Review.

Rosamond Hughes settled on St. Croix in 1989 after circumnavigating the world with her husband aboard their 42 foot cutter *Astrolabe*. She is one of the four original founders of The Writers' Circle of Saint Croix.

Marcia Jameson was born in Harlem, New York the child of Barbadian immigrants. She pursued the study of fine and commercial art specializing in illustration and graphic design, and has also illustrated several children's books. After re-locating to the Virgin Islands in 1978 Marcia worked as a free--lance artist in addition to her work at the Virgin Islands Department of Health, Division of Mental Health. "Looking for Bob Marley", based on a true adventure, is her literary maiden voyage.

Maud Pierre-Charles is a visual artist, native of Haiti, who lives and practices in St. Croix, US Virgin Islands and has maintained her art studio in the town of Christiansted since 1982.

Richard Arnon Mathews first enjoyed coming to St. Croix in 1968 and has been here since 1992. He received his bachelor's degree from Cornell in 1955 and graduated from Farleigh Dickinson, Teaneck, N.J. with a master's in English in 1975. A lifelong writer who has self-published two books, *CipherCopy* on grammar and *Reflections on Billy the Kid,* Mathews logged a quarter of a century as an advertising copywriter in NYC and a decade as an English teacher in New Jersey.

Alvin F. Rymsha is a retired engineer and, like several other writers who have contributed to this volume, was a transatlantic sailor. He prefers to write short stories as exemplified by his published "Sherlock Holmes: The Lost Cases," and the piece in this volume.

Priscilla Schneider, a school and medical librarian and writer, has been living on St. Croix since 1979. She has been fascinated with words since she first noticed letters jumping around on a page, due to her dyslexia.

Margery Tonks and her husband Bob sailed the seven seas on their 42 foot ketch *Seguin* for seventeen years after they retired from teaching. When the long-distance sailing adventure ended, they bought a house above Salt River on St. Croix and a 20 foot sailboat *Flicka of St. Croix*. Four years ago Bob passed away at age 97 when Marge was 90. Her current writings reflect the difficulty of adjusting to living without her beloved partner. They had been married for 67 years.

Made in the USA
Charleston, SC
04 November 2012